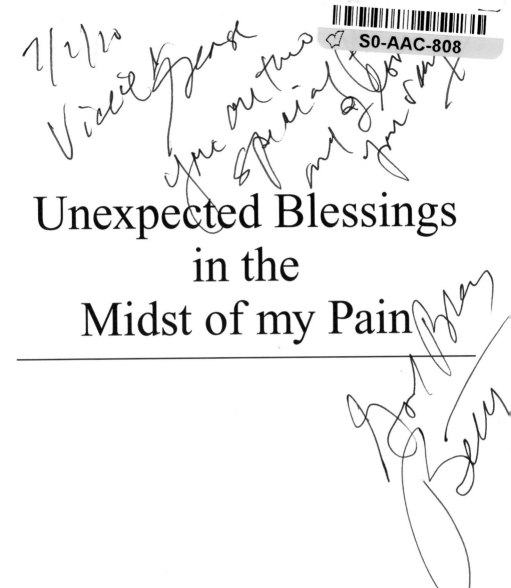

Unexpected Blessings
in the
Midst of my Pain

Betty M. Smith

Library of Congress Control Number:		2010902332
ISBN:	Hardcover	978-1-4500-4833-0
	Softcover	978-1-4500-4832-3
	Ebook	978-1-4500-4834-7

This book was printed in the United States of America.

To order additional copies of this book, contact:
Xlibris Corporation
1-888-795-4274
www.Xlibris.com
Orders@Xlibris.com
73742

CONTENTS

FOREWORD

Although I have just recently had the pleasure of meeting Betty Smith, I feel as if I have known her for a much longer period of time. I am a pretty good judge of people as I should be after so many years in medical practice and I would label Betty as one of the "good ones". She is a "shaker and a mover" and has really dedicated her life to helping others. I think that this is the main reason that she wrote this book. Betty felt by telling her story that she may be able to help others in the future who have experienced similar problems.

Betty Smith suffers from chronic headaches which have been diagnosed as occipital neuralgia. Occipital neuralgia is a headache syndrome that can have a multitude of causes such as osteoarthritis of the upper cervical spine, trauma to the occipital nerves, compression of the occipital nerves, cervical disc disease and many other causes related to medical conditions such as gout, diabetes, and vasculitis (inflammation of blood vessels). Although any of the above may be causes of occipital neuralgia, many cases can be attributed to chronically contracted neck muscles/neck tension or are idiopathic (unknown). A good medical workup for this problem is mandatory however in many cases, as I've mentioned, no specific pathology is found and the cause is labeled as being idiopathic meaning no one knows for sure what the cause is. That doesn't mean that there is no cause or that the patient is "crazy" . . . . .it only means that the etiology is very subtle. A caring knowledgeable health care professional . . . . .utilizing basic physiological principles . . . . in many cases can perform what appears to be a "miracle" to the patient. In searching for an answer to her persistent problem Betty happened upon Mike Jones's website and watched some video testimonials from his patients . . . . some of which I'm sure did seem "miraculous" to the patient.

Prior to my attending medical school I had the strong belief that medical care should be holistic. Holistic medicine, to me, implies working with the patient's "mind, body, and spirit". To really obtain a "healing" . . . . mind, body and spirit must be working together . . . . as one. A caring physician or any other ancillary health care provider can effect a tremendous positive influence on a patient just by the simple act of listening, or talking to the patient . . . . and by having the patient change what appears to be simple everyday life functions such as posture, instituting a proper diet, and an exercise program tailored to the patient's needs. Patient's are entitled to know what is in the mind of their treating physician and the health care provider and the patient have to work together as a team. This is the first step in the healing process. Confused and anxious patients only contribute negatively to their healing process . . . . so the patient must be informed and it is most important that the patient make a concentrated effort to relax. It has been know for a long time that fear causes tension and that tension produces pain. So just by the health care professional allaying one's fears, tension is reduced and thus so is pain. Unfortunately, common by—products of our modern world are fear and tension and one can see that no matter what is going on within our bodies, the problem can be greatly exacerbated by fear and tension. Thus if the patient has confidence in their treating health care professional . . . . that alone can help alleviate the fear of what is not known, and this is the first step in controlling one's pain. Most medical conditions are disease! A health care professional treating his patients holistically can remove the dis from dis-ease. In addition to being skilled in his specialty, Mike Jones in every sense of the word practices holistically and I feel that that is one of the main reasons for his success when dealing with difficult problems. I'm looking forward to seeing the result between Betty and Mike.

Leonard Knell, M.D., F.A.C.S.
Canton OH

INTRODUCTION

This book is dedicated to my mother, Mary Flowers Moore. When I was very young, she taught me that "living is giving." At 90 she still takes little and watches God make it much.

One of my favorite songs says, "Little means much when you place it in the Master's hand."

Mother is one of the most giving persons I have ever known. Her heart overflows with love reaching out to help and comfort while speaking words of encouragement and sharing her life's experiences.

She taught me to fight for things I believe in knowing that God would support me. I thank her for her wisdom, toughness and spirit of giving. And lastly, thank you Mother for keeping all seven of your children together when our father died. You were twenty-eight when many wanted to separate us. You very bravely stood up and said, "No one will ever separate my children. I will take care of all of them." God bless you.

Mary Flowers-Moore,
Betty's Mother

ACKNOWLEDGMENTS

Bishop Arthur M. Brazier. Thank you for taking me under your wings when I was eighteen and moved to Chicago from Logansport, Indiana. You have always been there for me and have taught me so much about life, community organizing, and being a good steward.

My entire family. Thank you for your support and prayers. You're always there for me whenever I need you.

My husband, Rev. Mark Smith. Thank you for your love, patience, prayers, strong faith in God and tender loving care.

Merrijo and Christopher McDaniel, my two children. Thank you. While not always understanding why I worked so hard, you supported me with your love and words of comfort.

Melissa Brown. Thank you. Even though busy, you fit me into your schedule to do the grammatical editing.

Nadine McIlwain-Massey. Thank you. Your experience, suggestions and candid comments have guided me through my first book. You are the best.

Marsha Brumfield-Jeffries. Thank you. You did my final review and made necessary corrections. I appreciate you.

My Holistic Health Practitioners

Barbara Bellassai. Thank you. You are such a caring massotherapist. I enjoy my time with you and appreciate the extra step you always take to help me.

Dr. Scott Snow, my Canton Chiropractor. Thank you. You always fit me into your schedule even if it is on the special day you spend with your baby girl. Thank you so much.

Dr. Dennis Prowell. Thank you. You have "anointed" hands and a wonderful sense of humor. Thank you for always fitting me into your schedule whenever I'm in Chicago.

Linda Clifton. Thank you for your friendship, special care and concern for my health. You take that extra step for me whenever I call.

Mark Crank, my Physical Therapist. Thank you. You have the magic touch, patience, words of wisdom and a kind smile. Thank you for reminding me to "take care of myself."

Janet Hawkins. Thank you. You have been such a dear friend and great herbalist for the past seven years. I appreciate you.

My greatest thanks are to my Lord and Savior Jesus Christ who has never failed me and continues to love me in spite of my shortcomings. **My daily prayer is and always has been, "Lord open doors that I need opened and give me favor. Keep closed the doors I should not walk through."**

UNEXPECTED DISMISSAL

I was born May 9, 1940 in Logansport Indiana. My birth name was Betty Lou Flowers. When I turned 18, I stopped using my middle name. After I graduated from High School in 1958, I moved to Chicago IL. This book is about events in my life from 1995 to April, 2010.

1995 was a very challenging year. Having been discharged from an agency where I had given 28 years of dedicated service, I was in total shock when I was told my services were no longer needed. There was a major misunderstanding about duties, staff, etc. and . . . . What I later learned was this was all a part of God's plan for my life; an "**UNEXPECTED BLESSING in the Midst of my Pain.**"

I thought after 28 years of working diligently, creating programs on a shoe string budget, comforting families, overcoming obstacles of racism, being surrounded by wonderful co-workers, believing and supporting the agency's mission, and, at the time, an understanding and caring boss, my job was very secure. It was secure until 1991 when God instructed me to open a recovery home for women and women with children recovering from drugs and alcohol.

Originally I was going to start my own not-for-profit agency in order to make sure that God's plan for this program would be followed. However, after meeting with the Director of Administrative Services and getting assurance that I would not face any obstacles, I decided to establish the program in my current department.

God began to give me daily detailed instructions that led to the opening of this program. He also gave me the name "Forever Free." I was truly in an area that was unfamiliar and had to totally rely on God for each step. The details of this program will be revealed in another book I'm writing entitled "Forever Free—The Home that Faith Built". When God gave me the directive to open this home, He already had the plan. All I needed to do was follow it.

My supervisor and the agency administrators were pleased and excited about the establishment of this program. However, they thought it would take me five years before the home would open. The home opened Monday, April 13, 1992. I shall never forget this date because a major water main burst in downtown Chicago.

Within a short time after the home was opened in 1992, I received a lot of publicity from the media; Oprah's camera crew came to the facility; Deloris Jordan took a special interest in the children and Halle Berry met with me and the women in our program to assist in the research for her movie "Loosing Isaiah". Things were going quite well until I was called into a meeting announcing that the agency administrators were going to transfer me and the program into another department.

I began to have concerns about whether or not my new supervisor would fully understand the operation of this God-given project and my role within the project. Her style of management was totally different from my former supervisor. She did not want me to be involved in the day-to-day operation but rather, she expected me to be responsible for strictly fundraising and supervising the Program Director. While this was the way her other programs operated, I was not comfortable with turning this new program completely over to the Program Director.

After many meetings and trying to conform to my supervisor's wishes as well as working long hours at the home; sometimes spending the night, I became very distraught and tired.

I talked to the Lord about my pain, concern and weariness. The struggle between me and my supervisor ended with a letter of termination effective October 5, 1995. Wow, was I in shock. I was 55 years old, had devoted my last 28 years creating programs and services for families and children and had very little money in my savings account.

After discussing this with Rev. Willie Barrow from Operation Push, she called the agency Executive Director to inquire about my termination. The Director agreed that a meeting should be scheduled to work out a termination package. Within a few weeks Rev Barrow and my friend Byron Brazier, met with Catholic Charities' personnel director and my former supervisor to negotiate a settlement. I was pleased with the results of this negotiation. However, I had feelings of anxiety and embarrassment. I had never been terminated from a job before.

For several days I moped around the house trying to figure out what God was doing. I know that nothing just happens. There is always a reason. But what could be the reason? My days seemed dark and long. I remember driving down Michigan Avenue on a bright and sunny day and all I could see was blackness. "Oh my goodness what is happening to me," I thought. "This is simply terrible; how will I get out of this state of depression. Dear God where are you?"

There were evenings when I would get in my car and drive for miles trying to collect my thoughts. One morning I awoke and convinced myself that perhaps I should try to do some freelance work. I prepared packets of information to do some counseling and workshops for other agencies based on my 28 years of experience in social services. I mailed out 100 packets of social work consultant material and did not receive one response. I then thought I would teach a workshop about stress using my experience as an exercise instructor. I received one call and after completing the workshop, received an excellent response from those in attendance. Because of this response, I thought more business would soon follow—wrong! No further calls were received.

My feelings of weariness, sadness and sometimes defeat became so intense that I would sit and stare at my computer unable to even turn it on. Once again I said, "God what are you telling me?" I was totally unable to function.

My Pastor, Bishop Arthur M. Brazier, knew I was depressed over losing a program that I created and was so dear to me. He said "Betty, God used you as a vessel to start this program. It does not belong to you. Your time was up, so He had to move you out of the way so He can give you another assignment." While I deeply love and respect Bishop, who was more like a father to me than a pastor, I just could not receive what he was saying. I said to myself, "How could God possibly give me something any better than Forever Free?" I was soon to find out.

I was able to keep my true feelings of sadness and defeat from my family and friends. When I was around them, I always put a smile on my face and pretended as if everything was okay.

It seemed that when I was at my lowest, Bishop's son, Byron, would call and say, "Betty, Dad said to check on you." I would then burst into tears as he talked to me and gave me words of encouragement. God always sends you what you need just when you need it most.

"Team in Training" My Patient Hero

When 1996 rolled in, I was still upset, somewhat angry, feeling sad and wondering how I was going to be able to move forward. I continued to pray, asking God for direction. I remember my Mother used to say "God helps those that help themselves". So with this in mind, it was necessary for me to quit having a pity party and do something that would be fulfilling and healthy for me and for someone else.

As a child I loved sports and when I would feel lonely or needed a lift I would run, walk, play tag football with the fellas and even climb trees. Now what could I possibly do that would be fulfilling for me and someone else?

For several weeks I gave this question a lot of thought. One morning while reading the newspaper, my eyes glanced on an ad for the Chicago Marathon. Well, I knew I was not a runner and, therefore, running was out of the question. On another page there was information connected with the Chicago Marathon but it was sponsored by the Leukemia Foundation and was referred to as "Team in Training." According to the article, you could either run or walk. Now, I loved to walk so the next day I called the Foundation. After receiving the necessary information, I decided to become a member of "Team in Training!" Wow what a major step. I always loved exercise and at one time owned an exercise studio "Stretchnastics." However, I had never walked a marathon, 26.2 miles. I thought, "Oh my goodness that's quite a distance."

It's ironic that I chose to walk a marathon. My mind goes back to when I was growing up in Logansport, Indiana. I had said that my Mother was one of the fastest walkers on the planet. It was very difficult for my siblings and me to keep up with her when we were walking together. She would always say, "You children are walking too slow, keep up with me." In my mind I would say, "Why don't you slow down." Of course this thought had to stay in my mind because if I had said it out loud my Mother would have given me one of her looks that said "I'll take care of you when I get home." And I definitely knew what that meant. Ouch! Many years later when I learned about race-walking I said, "My Mother was the originator of this great activity."

Anyway let's get back to my "Team in Training."

After I signed up and attended a "Team in Training" orientation, I was assigned a "patient hero", someone that had Leukemia. Each team member was required to collect a minimum of $1,000 in donations that would be used for Leukemia research. After the orientation, I gave this 26.2 mile walk a lot of thought and finally decided I couldn't possibly do it. I was 56 years old and had never walked more than four miles at any given time. I felt I was physically fit, but not enough to walk this marathon.

After receiving the name and information of my patient hero, Lisa Walters, age 12, I wanted to meet her. When I made the call to inquire how to make this happen I was told she was in the hospital.

Upon my arrival at the hospital I was greeted with a big, wonderful smile from this fragile, beautiful young lady who, in spite of the many tubes in her body and the loss of hair, said, "Thank you so much for walking the marathon for me—God bless you!" After that, how could I not walk this marathon? Lisa didn't realize it, but she inspired me and I immediately began my training with the team. She was truly a **BLESSING** for me just when I needed it.

My training with the team was a wonderful experience and put me in touch with so many great people who were walking for "patient heroes." There were approximately 150 walkers. I was told we were the only ones that were permitted to walk this Chicago Marathon; the others had to be runners. Since that time, there are many walkers that participate to raise money for many worthwhile programs.

It was rather chilly the day of the walk, but everyone was upbeat and ready for the challenge. We started two hours before the runners. I noticed some of the walkers decided to start with a light jog, probably to keep warm because it was pretty chilly at 6:00 in the morning. I was not prepared to jog. My mind was set for a 26.2 walk, so I stuck to this.

It was exciting to see the many people on the sidelines cheering and chanting words of encouragement. One lady shouted and pointed to me, "looking good, keep going". Those words made me feel very special. The music was playing, energy was flowing and there were plenty of bananas, oranges and water on the route. It was a beautiful, bright sunny day.

Betty walking Chicago Marathon—1997

To show you how inexperienced I was, I had a pouch around my waist that was loaded with a lot of what I thought were necessary items such as my billfold, DVD's, snacks, Kleenex and a few other items. I also had on headphones, two t-shirts and two sweatshirts. As I began my walk with CeCe Winans' music playing through the headphones, I began to feel very, very heavy so I started to shed clothes. There were sweatshirts and other items thrown along the route, so this let me know that it was okay to peel off some of my clothing.

When I entered my 11th mile I saw my sister Judy and my girlfriend Bobbi on the trail and immediately handed them my pouch, headphones and anything else that was weighing me down. My girlfriend Bobbi, who has such a great sense of humor, decided to give me some serious encouragement. She started shouting "Go Betty, you can do it." She ran beside me with her long, black wig flying in the wind, and breathing heavily as her arms were frantically waiving. After she ran a half-block she said "Well, you're on your own. I'm completely worn out." She had the other spectators roaring with laughter. She was simply hilarious.

Five hours and 50 minutes later I crossed the finish line. I walked the entire 26.2 miles. Much to my surprise the first person I saw after crossing the line was my "patient hero" Lisa, sitting in her wheelchair surrounded by her wonderful family. That made it all worthwhile.

Walking the marathon was such an enjoyable experience that I walked the entire marathon again in 1997. Lisa, again, was my "patient hero".

Lisa is an accomplished pianist and song writer. She is now doing music research in another country. She has written a book about her challenges with Leukemia. Lisa and I correspond on a regular basis. She was an **"UNEXPECTED BLESSING in the Midst of my Pain."**

I continued to stay busy, going through the motions, in spite of my depression. God was with me, but I didn't understand why He was allowing me to suffer. I remember a Jamaican friend of mine, Signa, saying to me, "Betty, if you haven't sweat blood like Jesus, you should not complain." Sometimes just repeating this to myself helped me get through the day.

After the marathon I needed to continue staying busy. Bishop was always mindful of the importance of physical fitness, so two days a week the church rented the neighborhood YWCA. I became the Aerobic Director and worked closely with Coach Stevens who was the Physical Fitness Director.

I had 40 plus students who faithfully participated in the classes. It was a joy for me to not just teach the classes but to interact with a lot of them about taking care of their bodies "the temple of the Holy Spirit." I then started a "Back to Basics" class on healthy lifestyles.

In addition to teaching the exercise classes, I was Director of the Singles' Ministry for the church.

I was responsible for working with the committee and planning events for the thousands of singles that were in the church. Some of the activities included quarterly meetings with our Bishop that incorporated a question and answer session. Singles were allowed to ask him any question as long as it was in "good taste." The singles felt quite comfortable asking Bishop questions in an open forum knowing they would not be embarrassed or criticized.

Questions like "Is it okay to kiss a Christian Single" were asked. While some of the singles thought this was a very simple and perhaps childish question, the person asking it was a new member of the church and wanted to make sure he was in line with what Bishop was teaching. Some of the other questions involved oral sex and homosexuality. If being a Christian means you can't talk to your Pastor about these things, then who should you talk to about them? Bishop was very up front and sometimes very humorous with the group as he scratched his head, put his hand on his chin, looked up to God and answered the very pointed questions that were troubling the singles.

We also had midnight boat cruises on Lake Michigan with lots of tasty food and great gospel music; a Super Bowl party every January; a summer picnic; day long workshops with experienced facilitators and speakers such as Dr. Carolyn Showell from Baltimore, Maryland and Dr. Noel Jones from Los Angeles, California.

Some of the singles would call me for advice as they were struggling with challenges in a relationship, or not, at this particular time, wanting to start a new relationship. The men needed to know a polite way to tell the women they were just not ready without them thinking they were gay.

The majority of the men that called were either recently divorced or just coming out of a bad relationship. They expressed to me that they needed time to heal and focus on the word of God. Some of the women were lonely and yes, some depressed, because they felt as if their time clock was winding down.

The Apostolic Church of God was definitely a "household name" and known for the number of good looking, Bible toting, well dressed men in attendance. One evening in the locker room at the health club, I overheard ladies discussing this very topic. One of them said, "Girl if you want to find yourself a good looking, clean cut, Christian man, go to the Apostolic Church of God." Bishop was such a wonderful male role model. His very presence and demeanor attracted men that looked up to him as a powerful leader.

It was in my role as Director of the Singles' Ministry that Bishop introduced me to Michele Hoskins who became a very dear friend of mine. We would take long walks along the lake front, chat about our children, and join some of our other girlfriends for lunch. Michele later became the Founder of Michele Foods and has appeared on the cover of all major business magazines. If you want to taste great syrup, check out Michele at *www.michelefoods.com.*

Even though I was having my challenges and trying to find my way, it was necessary for me to stay prayerful and ask God for direction as these singles called me for guidance. The men and women that called were always very respectful of me and trusted what I would say to them.

Every day I would talk with God trying to work through my challenges and feelings of hopelessness. He would continue to say the same thing, "REST!" I didn't know how to rest! I had always been a very busy person, sometimes working as many as three jobs while raising my children.

After God repeatedly told me to "Rest," I quit fighting it and said, "Okay God, I give up I will try to do just that." I began to pray more, watch television, which is something I rarely had time to do, and even cook, which was something I never did once my children were grown and moved away. Now if you would talk to my children about my cooking they would say, "We always knew when mommy cooked the food" and then they would snicker. You guessed it, cooking was not one of my strengths.

I had a part-time housekeeper, but decided it would be better if I cleaned my house. This was definitely not the person I used to be, but God was truly working something out in my life.

In July, 1997, I was invited to lead an exercise class at my church's sanctuary choir retreat. I prayed that God would give me exactly what to do and say in order to meet the needs of those attending.

I selected a powerful song, "Count on Me" by Whitney Houston and CeCe Winans, taken from the movie "Waiting to Exhale" as our exercise song. Some of the lyrics are: "I can see it's hurting you, I can feel your pain, it's hard to see the sunshine through the rain, I know sometimes it seems as if it's never going to end, but you'll get through it, just don't give in. Count on me through thick and thin a friendship that will never end, when you are weak I will be strong helping you to carry on, call on me, I will be there, don't be afraid, just believe me when I say, count on me."

These words meant a lot to me and I wanted to share them with everyone on the Retreat.

I can't really explain to you exactly what happened, but I know that God began to speak through me and I relayed a message of forgiveness, love and hope to those in attendance. I told them to go to three people, hug them, give them words of encouragement and tell them, "You can count on me!" Immediately after I spoke this and they put into action what I instructed, the tears began to flow from the choir members, the praises to God went up and I felt such a "release" from my state of depression that it was simply MIRACULOUS. I felt as if a heavy weight was removed from my shoulders. My eyes closed and then opened with seemingly new sight. Everything in the room appeared brighter. I began to rejoice and thank God for the release and for the "**UNEXPECTED BLESSING in the Midst of my Pain**."

A few months later, I awoke out of a dream that was so real. I sat up in the bed, squinted my eyes, looked around the room and allowed the dream to replay itself in my head. In the dream I saw myself in a small town working and enjoying it! Huh? I said "God are you sending me back to my hometown?" My hometown, Logansport, Indiana, has a population of less than 25,000, and very few African-Americans. I didn't even wait for God to answer. My next thought was "Wherever you send me Lord, I'll go." I knew this was the time to completely surrender to whatever God had planned for my journey.

1998—IT'S WORTH THE WAIT FOR A MATE!

One afternoon in January, 1998, a friend and I sat at my dining room table talking and preparing packets for my exercise workshops. After an hour or more had passed I excused myself from the table and walked down the stairs to check the mail box. Along with bills and some advertisements was a letter from Canton, Ohio. The return address had Mark M. Smith. For a few seconds I just looked at the envelope and repeated his name several times trying to get a picture of who he was. Then a light bulb went off and I could see his face. In my mind I was trying to figure out why, after all these years, he would write me a letter.

Before climbing the stairs to return to the dining room table, I read the letter. It was one paragraph long but said, "Hi do you remember me? Good. I met you at the 'shut in' at your church in 1991. You were leading the ladies on an early morning walk. I'm coming to Chicago and would like to take you to dinner." His phone number was at the top of the letter.

I felt a bit of excitement but also had so many questions going on in my head. Upon returning to the table, I told my friend about the letter. She had many questions. How long had I known him? When was the last time I had spoken with him? etc. I told her about meeting him at the church retreat in 1991. A good friend of his, Rick "Soup" Campbell, invited him to our annual retreat. At the Retreat, Mark mentioned he was retired and lived in Canton, Ohio. I said to myself, "Canton, Ohio, that sounds boring."

Then my mind reflected back in time when Bishop and our singing group would travel to churches where he would be the guest speaker and our group would sing. One of our trips led us to the Bethel Apostolic Church in Canton where Eld. Robert McMurray was Pastor. It was so long ago I can't remember much about Canton except it appeared to be very small!

Back to the Retreat. After reflecting back in time about my trip to Canton, I pictured Mark in a small little house sitting by himself in a very retired state. I immediately dismissed any thoughts of me visiting him or staying in touch. At this particular time in my life I was enjoying my work and busy preparing to open the women's recovery home, an assignment God had given me earlier in the year. I did not have time to think about a relationship or telephone calls.

I read Mark's letter several times and wondered why after all of these years he decided to contact me. This is what happens when God is in control!

After receiving the letter, we spoke on the phone for several weeks. It was so strange because it was as if we had known one another all our lives. We laughed, shared stories, and acted like teenagers.

Each time we talked I felt so much love in my heart for him. It was rather frightening. I remember saying, "God why are you giving me so much love for a man that I don't really know?" God's response was, "I know him." Wow, that blew me away!

One day during our phone conversation he said, "What are you doing for Valentine's Day?" I said "I have nothing planned!" He said, "Then why don't I come up and take you out to dinner." I said, "Fine!"

Well, needless to say, I was excited and giddy waiting for Mark to visit me in Chicago. I talked to my girlfriend, Bobbi, and in a way that only she can say it; her words were, "I think he cometh seeking a wife." I said, "It is nothing like that Bobbi. We are just reacquainting ourselves with one another. It's been a long time." She just looked at me and laughed.

Mark was due in Chicago on February 13th at 3:00 p.m. At 10:00 a.m. my phone rang and he said, "I'm here!" I couldn't believe it. I was not ready. I had made an appointment at the beauty shop and had a few other things planned before he arrived. Anyway, I said, "Oh wonderful. Why don't you come over and we can chat, but I have some things I must do before noon.

When he walked up the stairs I remember so vividly opening the door and looking at him with one leg on one step and his other long leg stretched on the top step. He had a big smile on his face and said, "Hi!" He had such a warm smile and his head was bald. When I first met him he had hair. Well, he had some hair! I really liked the bald look and he was "kinda cute!"

We talked for a while about me and then him, sharing a few stories. I learned he was not just a minister, as he was when I met him in 1991, but was now the Pastor of a small church. In my mind I said, "A Pastor, oh my goodness." I never wanted to date a minister and definitely not a Pastor. I told him that I had to leave for the beauty shop but he could make himself comfortable until I returned. He seemed like a very nice, kind, trustworthy person, and after all he was a Pastor, so I felt I could leave him in my house until I returned.

I also shared with him a copy of "GOSPEL TODAY" magazine that contained an article on me. This article talked about my leadership of the Apostolic Church of God Singles' Ministry. It was the Valentine's Day issue.

When I returned from the beauty shop, we talked for another hour, exchanging stories of our lives. My friend Bobbi said she wanted to prepare dinner for us and I agreed. She said, "You know men love good food, so I'll fix you something very special." She also knew that I was not a very good cook and figured if I cooked the meal he would never come back. She told me she was going to fix her "signature peach cobbler." Bobbi was known for this famous dessert and some times would bake as many as 20 at a time and give them to her friends.

Mark and I enjoyed Bobbi's meal, especially the "peach cobbler." He was a bit tired from the long drive, so we decided to end our evening early so he could return to his hotel and get a good night's sleep.

The next day I asked him what he would like to do. He loves good bread so I took him to the north side and we visited three bread shops. Yummy! We later went to Navy Pier, shopped and had a great lunch. We were like two giddy kids having the time of our lives. What a wonderful feeling!

After we left Navy Pier, Mark drove me home and went to his hotel to rest before returning to pick me up for our Valentine's dinner.

Several hours later he returned, looking very dapper and carrying a beautiful bouquet of flowers. How sweet! I took him to what I thought was a nice and fun place to eat. I learned four years later that he did not like the food or atmosphere. However, he loved the company. We had a wonderful time even though we shared the table with several other couples. I chose a Japanese Restaurant where food is cooked at your table.

I asked him what prompted him to call me after six years of not hearing from me. He said, "I was praying and God gave me clarity that it was time to call you." Wow, that nearly knocked me over, but also let me know that God was definitely in whatever was to happen between the two of us. He also had the business card I had given him in 1991. It was a little crumpled but he had it!

After dinner we returned to my home where we continued talking and sharing information about our lives. It was so natural but seemed unreal that we were so freely sharing and enjoying one another's company. Somewhere during our hours of conversation, he proposed to me! He said, "I believe I've made a commitment to you, but you must talk to God to find out how to respond and whatever He says, that is what we'll do." Then he said, "I know I can take care of me but had not thought about taking care of a wife." His next sentence was, "I don't know if I can live in Chicago but maybe so." Without hesitation and wondering where it came from, I said, "I can move to Canton!" We talked a little longer and then he departed.

As soon as he left and the door closed I heard God say, "That is your husband!" The anointing of God was so powerful it knocked me backwards down my long hallway and I began to rejoice. I knew this was God! This was definitely an **"UNEXPECTED BLESSING in the Midst of my Pain."** This was such a powerful night that even as I'm typing this part of my book and reflecting back on that night, I can feel the presence of God filling my heart with warmth and love. So very POWERFUL!

The next morning I met Mark for breakfast and he looked across the table at me with his "big" eyes and said, "What did God say?" I said to him, "You know what God said!" He said, "Yes I do. God said you are to come to Canton and be my wife!" We were both so very, very happy and excited. He left for Canton and I went to church.

I shared my good news with my friend Dr. Helen Barge, now Vallier. She said, "Oh, Betty this is wonderful!" She then said, "I think this is going to be more than a marriage. God has other plans for you!" Dr. Vallier has always been one of my dear friends and one that I can always expect to tell me like it is. She is always on target with a message from God.

The next person I saw was my sister Judy. When I told her, the expression on her face was one of shock and disbelief. She stood there shaking her head, trying to collect her thoughts and then said, "Oh, you must be kidding. I think I need a drink!" When she said "drink," I knew she was upset because she doesn't drink unless it is a little dinner wine with her meal.

My mind reflected back on the dream about moving to a small town. I said to myself, "Well, it isn't Logansport, Indiana but Canton, Ohio. I hope and pray Canton is larger than Logansport." I then thought, Canton, Ohio, the place I chuckled about in 1991 was soon to be my home.

I remember so many times when talking to God about what kind of husband I would like to have the next time I marry. My first marriage lasted 16 years and gave me two wonderful children, Merrijo and Christopher. I had been divorced 18 years and learned that Mark had been divorced for 25 plus years. Wow, look at God!

Bishop taught us to be SPECIFIC when asking God for something. He also gave us an example that if you ask God for a Cadillac and someone wants to give you a smaller, less expensive car, then it didn't come from

God so don't take it, but wait on God. This is great advice but sometimes difficult to take.

Before meeting Mark, I had my share of disappointed relationships. I thought about Bishop's sermon on being specific so I made a list of what I wanted in my next husband.

When I would speak to God about my next husband I made it very, very clear what I wanted:

a) Someone that loved Him;
b) A very tall man with nice broad shoulders; I don't know why but I have a thing for broad shoulders☺
c) Someone that loved to workout, go to the gym, walk, etc.;
d) He had to have means to take care of himself and me, even though I wanted to work and help;
e) A nice ranch home with lots of windows where I could see trees and grass and water; My condo in Chicago had 14 rooms but I could only see out the front and back. The side windows were very close to other condos. There was absolutely no view, a very small backyard and no front yard.
f) Nice in-laws.

I remember one person that I dated had four of the six qualities I had prayed for. He was very nice and quite a gentleman. I said to myself, "Hmmm, maybe this is the one." He had most of the things I prayed for, so I began to pay more attention to the relationship.

Well, this person saw that look in my eye and said to me, "God told me we are to be friends." At first I was somewhat angry but I thought about what I had prayed for and there were two things missing from my description of what I wanted in a husband so I knew he was "not the one!" I believe God gave the gentleman the message because he saw I had put myself in a position where I might have ignored it if He had spoken to me. The gentleman and I went out a few times after that and then decided it would be best not to continue dating. We remained friends.

How many times do we date someone and when one or the other ends the relationship we become upset, antagonistic, crazy and sometimes go into a state of depression? The Bible teaches that whatever state we are in, we are, therefore, to be content. This is sometimes very, very difficult but this is where we must really rely on God to help get us through difficult situations.

Sometimes when we are lonely or feel that right person will never surface; there is oftentimes a temptation to settle for Mr. or Miss Wrong. The key is to wait on God knowing that He will give us what we need when we need it. Ladies, Proverbs 18:22 says "Whoso findeth a wife findeth a good thing and obtains favor of the Lord." I know we are living in a day where women are very assertive, but God's word never changes! I also know that this is easier said than done.

When I first met Mark, I definitely was not ready for marriage and he probably wasn't either so it took seven years for God to get both of us ready. **IT WAS WORTH THE WAIT!**

Mark is a retired police officer, 6 feet 3 inches tall with big shoulders. He's a hunk. He works out at the gym three times a week, has a ranch home with a huge back yard, plenty of trees, flowers, a large fish pond and 6 wonderful brothers and sisters. Now did God hook me up or what? "We have not because we ask not!" Wait on the Lord and be of good courage! This was in February, 1998. We planned our wedding for April 18, 1998.

I decided not tell too many people that day, so I just rejoiced and thanked God for this wonderful **BLESSING** in my life.

The next day I called my children and told them about Mark. Right away my son said, "Mom, I want to talk to him!" I became a little upset about this because, after all, I was grown! When I mentioned this to Mark, he said, "Your son is just being protective and he should talk to me!"

My daughter had many questions but when I told her Mark was 65; she breathed a sigh of relief. She thought he was some young man when I described how he looked and worked out at the gym, etc. My children and Sister Judy have always been very protective of me and suspicious of anyone they felt was remotely interested in me. They did not want to see me hurt or taken advantage of—as if I couldn't take care of myself!

They have gone as far as check financial reports, police records, investigate businesses and companies, etc., to make sure the person interested in me was solid!

My son was not the only one concerned, Mark's son, Mark II, whose nickname is "Biff", called me. We had a pleasant conversation and he welcomed me to the family.

WEDDING PLANS

The following week I called a group of my friends, told them about my upcoming marriage and invited them to my home for a meeting. All of them showed up and on time! They had a long list of questions about Mark. Where and how we met? When did he propose? They wanted every little detail, especially my single girlfriends. After I answered all of their questions, I discussed my need for their help in planning this major event.

Each person was given an assignment such as logistics, invitations, reception, etc. They chuckled and one of them said, "You're giving us assignments like you used to give your staff." We all had a good laugh. These were truly some wonderful friends who put my mind at ease that they would follow through on their assignments to make this a wonderful wedding day.

When I called Vanessa, wedding coordinator at the church, and gave her the good news and the date, her reply was, "Betty, you know I need a six month or longer window because of all of the weddings we have." I said, "Vanessa, this is the date I need so please see what you have available." Well, as God would have it, at that time, there was nothing on the books for April 18th! She was in shock.

My biggest hurdle was to talk to Bishop, my pastor, stand-in-dad, and friend. He was scheduled to be out of town for a few days so I decided to wait until he returned. Upon his return, I made an appointment to inform him about my forthcoming wedding. I was a bit nervous about this meeting knowing that Bishop was going to put on his "serious" father's hat.

My mind went back to when I was 19 and my mother said to Bishop, "Please take care of my daughter. She is very young and was raised in a small, country town. She will need a lot of support." He assured her he would watch after me.

At one time I was Bishop's personal secretary at the church and later became Secretary of the Official Board. I was one of the first women to be a board member. Bishop, his wife and children treated me like family. This meant a lot to me and my mother.

Now back to my meeting with Bishop. My first words were, "Bishop, please hear me out before you comment."

After I finished he said, "Betty, I'm happy for you and wish you the best but I think you need to wait until you get to know this man a little better." I then began to tell Bishop how God was working in my life and a few of the details leading up to the proposal. I felt that what I went through in losing my job, the depression, and my dream, how Mark and I met, etc., that this was God's way of preparing me for this next big step in my life.

Bishop then said, "Betty, I do believe God is in this. I believe you have just had a 'Job' experience." For those of you who might not understand this comment, 'Job' from the Bible—read his story. The moral, "The Lord giveth and the Lord taketh away, blessed be the name of the Lord." When God takes something from you, He often restores that which was taken and gives you more.

Betty, Bishop Brazier and Mark

Bishop then said, "Now Betty you know that I must officiate this ceremony and I'm sure my calendar is booked for that date." He then pulled out his little black book. As busy as he is, Bishop has always scheduled his appointments. I was always impressed and fascinated by this. When he looked at his book, he then glanced at me. In my mind I said oh, he must have it completely booked. Instead, with his brow wrinkled and a look of amazement on his face, he said, "I don't have anything in my book on that date!" Now I should have known that it was available. God is at work!

Mark and I were very busy. I had to fly to Cleveland, Ohio and meet his Bishop, J. Delano Ellis, II. Mark then had to fly to Chicago to meet with my Pastor, Bishop Brazier. Other trips included meeting his family in Canton and driving to Logansport to meet my mother.

My good friend, Kitty Daily, accompanied me on my first trip to Canton to meet Mark's family. They were delightful and Kitty and I had a wonderful time. My mind flashed back to another one of the items I listed when I asked God for a mate. I wanted my husband to have a wonderful family. I was especially excited to meet his Mother who was 90 years old. After she and I had talked for a while, she looked at me and said "Now don't you two start having babies right away." We both had a good laugh! This would have definitely been an Abraham and Sarah story.

During the meeting Mark and I had with Bishop Brazier, the Bishop said, "Betty, I give you two years and you will be busy working on a project in Canton." I said, "Bishop, I am retired!" I told God no more social work and no more music." I worked in the Music Department at the Apostolic Church of God for 30 years and in social work for 28 years. Bishop just looked at me and smiled.

Bishop then wrinkled his brow, as he often does, gave Mark a very stern and serious look and said, "Mark, if the marriage doesn't work, send her home." Mark immediately responded by saying, "Bishop, this is going to work, don't worry." All of us chuckled.

The meeting with Bishop Ellis was quite amusing. He had a serious look, but a great sense of humor. I thought it was so funny when he called his wife on the intercom and asked her to "come and see who Overseer brought home." At the time, my husband was an Overseer in the United Pentecostal Church of Christ Organization.

In between all of the meetings there was a lot to do such as selling my condo and deciding what to do with the majority of my furniture. Mark had a fully furnished beautiful home. However, he told me to bring several pieces of my furniture and anything else that would make me feel comfortable.

My wedding consisted of some of the most outstanding soloists from the Apostolic Church of God. My dear friend, Herald "Chip" Johnson, coordinated my music and played the organ even though he told me he no longer did weddings! Thanks again Chip. Singers included Dwayne Lee, Jimmy Hudson, Roberta Thomas and Elizabeth Norman. My Old and New Testament scriptures were read by Minister Byron Brazier. My son, Christopher, walked me down the aisle and through his tears responded when Bishop Brazier asked, "Who gives this woman to be wed?" My son said, "I do." He wiped his eyes with a hanky that Bishop Ellis had handed him and took his seat.

Friends and relatives came from as far away as Las Vegas and as close as Logansport, Indiana to make this a day I shall never forget.

Our reception was emceed by yet another dear friend, Ivory Nuckolls. She surprised me with one of my favorite pianists, Randy Johnson.

Many in attendance told me it was one of the most inspirational and anointed weddings they had ever attended commenting that they felt as if they had been to a "church service!"

Merrijo, Christopher and Betty—1998

Mark and Betty—wedding photo 4-18-98

Only God could have orchestrated this major event in my life and for this, I am truly grateful.

My youngest sister, Judy, was still not happy about this marriage. Before entering the reception, she pulled my husband aside and said to him in her very stern and serious voice, "You make sure you take good care of my sister or you will hear from me!" Mark laughed and said, "You don't have to worry, I'm going to take good care of my wife."

He then said to me, "Don't worry, Judy and I will become the best of friends." He was right—today, they are the best of friends.

I always tell single men and women that are anxious for a mate. "**It's worth the wait.**" Make your request known to God and be very specific about what you want. Then, you must wait on him. If you ask for a Cadillac, do not settle for anything less. God's timing is not our timing!

In the fall of 1997, I had already planned one of my "alone vacations" in Puerto Vallarta, Mexico for the week of April 20th, 1998. The date for our wedding fit right into the plan and the best part—I was not alone! Mark and I had a romantic honeymoon with great weather and delicious Mexican and American food.

Family Photo—Betty and Mark's wedding

MY MOVE TO CANTON, OHIO

After the honeymoon I moved to Canton. The first three months were spent introducing me to Canton, enjoying the many restaurants and just getting to know one another. Mark's family gave us another reception so I could meet some of his friends.

It was quite an adjustment for both of us since we were used to living alone. We had to learn how to share all facets of our life that included washing and folding clothes. Now this was something that took quite an adjustment on my part. Mark was a very neat person and I was not as neat. He had the military training and everything had to be in order!

Cooking was not one of my strengths so we did a lot of eating out. One day I fixed chicken, mashed potatoes, gravy, mixed vegetables and baked a cake. Whew! I was tired. When we sat down to eat, Mark looked at me with his big eyes and a smile on his face and said, "Honey, you don't have to work this hard in the kitchen, we have a very nice deli at Fisher Foods." I could have strangled him!

Mark loved to snack on ice cream, candy and sometimes cookies while watching TV. Of course I snacked with him. However, this was not good for my size 8 figure. Little by little I started gaining weight. I had always been able to maintain my weight and size but not now! I remember when I had my exercise studio in Chicago talking to some of my newly wed students about not dropping out of class and neglecting their health. The majority of them continued coming but the pounds were adding up. Eventually some of them dropped out and when I would see them at church or at a restaurant, they would try to hide their heads in shame. I would just shake my head and say, "Shame on you, you were not that heavy when you married. Don't get upset if your hubby starts complaining." Well, I was beginning to understand the challenge.

Mark and Betty resting after working out at the health club

My lifestyle was totally different. I was definitely not used to eating a lot of fried foods, desserts, potatoes, and other starchy foods. These are some of the things my husband could eat and not gain a pound! On the other hand, I continued to gain. In the first seven years, I gained a whopping 25 pounds. Disgusting! My Chicago friends and some of my family thought I looked so much better with the extra weight and tried to discourage me from dieting. It wasn't until my 11th year of being married that I decided that the extra pounds had to go!

After being in Canton for three months, I decided to make a few phone calls and find out a little about the social service network. I made appointments with some of the major social service agency Executive Directors to introduce myself. At that time I had no intention of opening a social service agency. I was retired. As if I didn't already know, once again it was going to be brought back to me that you do not tell God what you are or are not going to do. You'll soon see how much I was not in control.

I met with Mike Johnson, Executive Director of Child and Adolescent Services; Jim Bridges, Founder/Executive Director of Pathways Caring for Children; and, Dan Fuline, Executive Director of Community Services. At that time it was Catholic Community Services. Dan reflected on what he termed as one of the best Catholic Charities conferences he ever attended and said it was in Chicago. When he said this, it automatically opened a big door for us to communicate. Not long after meeting Dan, I was invited to become a member of the Community Services' board. This was very exciting and gave me an opportunity to meet so many wonderful people. I was one of the first non-Catholic members of his board and was a member for six years.

My next phone call was to the United Way to inquire about a social service network. I thought it would be good to occasionally attend a meeting of the various social service agencies. This call put me in touch with a young lady named Susan Day (not her real name), Founder/Executive Director of a social service agency. The contact was a very good one. Susan was quite knowledgeable about the ins and outs of the social work arena, particularly as it related to the African-American population in Stark County.

I continued making contacts with various social service agencies which gave me a great perspective on the kinds of programs and services that were offered in Stark County.

In August I was a bit restless and my husband and I both thought perhaps I should look for a part-time job to keep me occupied. It would also bring in some extra dollars to help with vacations and some of our other "wants!"

While working in Chicago, one of my responsibilities was supervising a Senior Work Experience Program so I checked to see if Canton had a Senior Program or something similar. I was excited to find out that such an office existed. I made an appointment and completed an application. When they reviewed it, they were pleased to see my extensive background in working with seniors. After several meetings, they asked if I would allow the local newspaper to interview me. I agreed and was very surprised when asked if they could photograph me in my home. I made the front page!

I, once again, contacted the Senior Employment Office and was introduced to Colleen Cramblett-Oneill, producer of their television program. She asked if I would be a guest and talk about my move from Chicago to Canton. I graciously accepted.

The station WCTV was in Wadsworth, Ohio (21 miles from Canton) and was supported by the City. I thought this was a pretty neat thing and wondered why Canton did not have something similar. After my interview I was approached by Johanna Perrino, the stations Operations and Community Relations Coordinator, who asked if I would like to have a show of my own! She said, "I'll produce it for you." How could I pass up an opportunity like this? While living in Chicago, I had a cable TV show so this was not a new experience.

My show is called "On Track with Betty Mac." The format focuses on healthy living, neighborhood development, social service information, community events and anything that is positive.

Mark and Betty with TV Award

When I began taping my TV show, I had a segment that highlighted individuals that were making a difference in the community. As I began to learn about the many wonderful people in Canton, contacts were made asking if they would consider being saluted on my show. One of Canton's jewels is Debbie Horn, a highly energetic, hard-working, friendly lady employed at Catholic Community Services. Her background sheet indicated that she was also a volunteer for the Pro Football Hall of Fame Festival so I immediately called to ask if she could put me in touch with the person in charge of the fashion show. Her immediate response was, "Not a problem, consider it done." The following week I received a letter with information regarding the next fashion show meeting. This is what I call Devine intervention.

In a later chapter, I will talk more about my wonderful experience with the Pro Football Hall of Fame Festival's Fashion Show.

After being on the air for approximately four months, my husband was given an opportunity to have a Bible Study TV Show. He is an excellent Bible teacher and this was a great way for him to share God's word with others. In our second year of programming, both of us won awards for best shows in our area of programming.

GOD GIVES ME A NEW ASSIGNMENT

Approximately six months after I moved to Canton, it was a Sunday morning and I was playing the organ at my husband's church. The congregation was singing one of those foot stompin' gospel songs and the spirit of God filled the place. After the singing stopped it was time for my husband to preach. While he was preaching, I heard a voice in my ear that said, "You cannot retire. There is too much work that needs to be done." I knew this was not my husband's voice and realized it was God speaking to me. I heard it, but I really did not want to receive it. I couldn't believe that God was asking me to come out of retirement and go back to work.

On Track with Betty Mac—TV show backdrop

When the Lord spoke to me, my mind reflected back to the conversation I had with Bishop Brazier during the meeting with Mark and me. He said, "Betty, I give you two years and you will be working on a project in Canton. You have been in training 40 years for Canton." I said to myself, "Bishop I'm retired."

The 40 year's Bishop mentioned was when I worked closely by his side in the Woodlawn neighborhood where his church is located. Bishop founded The Woodlawn Organization, a neighborhood that reminded me of the Summit neighborhood in Canton, except Summit did not have as many challenges. I encourage you to read Bishop Brazier's book, "The Woodlawn Organization, a story of Black Self-Determination." I had the honor of typing the manuscript for this book. I typed Bishop's book from a reel-to-reel tape using an IBM typewriter.

If you work or minister in the inner city, I would encourage you to learn more about Bishop's leadership of the Apostolic Church of God, a church that started with less than 100 members and now has more than 20,000. Log on to www.ACOG-Chicago.org. Bishop is now retired and his son Byron is the new Pastor.

The 40 years I worked with Bishop were profoundly challenging, inspiring and life-changing. Bishop was my spiritual father. I first met him at age 15 when he was conducting a revival at my church in Logansport. When I moved to Chicago he became my Pastor. When he became my Pastor, I remember my Mother saying to him, "Please take care of my daughter." And he promised he would and he did!

Because Bishop was such a major part of my life, for his 35th Anniversary as Pastor of the Apostolic Church of God, I decided to write a book of poetry that is quite humorous with art work by Marc Moran. In this book I reveal some things that many did not know about him. The book is titled, "Bishop Arthur M. Brazier, Man with a Vision." This book can be purchased at the Apostolic Church of God book store or by logging on to my website www.bettymac.org.

Book Cover

Now back to my story. After the Lord spoke to me about not retiring, my husband told me to use the small space in the back of the church for my office. The Summit Elementary School was two blocks from our church. My husband suggested I contact the school's Principal and get some information regarding the neighborhood. I made contact with Bob Vero, who at that time was the Principal. When I explained to him who I was and what I wanted to do in the neighborhood, he referred me to Darlene Leghart, President of Summit United Neighbors. Darlene and I chatted so we could learn about one another and how we might be able to work together. We soon discovered that both of us are passionate about people and neighborhoods.

In an effort to gather information about available grants, I visited the local library and found an extensive directory of local foundations. I was simply amazed by the large number. This information was relayed to Darlene who was not familiar with the foundations and she indicated she did not know how to write grants.

I expressed to her that grant writing was something new to me, but perhaps we could find one that would be easy to write.

My next research led me to an available grant opportunity with the Stark Community Foundation. They had money available for neighborhood organizations. I immediately informed Darlene. It was a rather easy process, so I wrote the grant and listed Darlene as the contact person. It was funded for $2,000.00.

I really did not want to start my own agency and I felt that working with someone else would satisfy my obligation to God's request. So, I talked with Susan about the Summit neighborhood and asked if she knew about any funding that might be available to help the residents. Susan invited me to an open meeting with Family Council of Stark County. She also advised me that she was not really interested in being involved in anything that required a lot of paperwork. I told her I would handle the paperwork but needed her to head up the project. Because Susan still had her agency to run, she asked that I attend the meetings to learn more about the funding.

After numerous meetings with Family Council, they announced that anyone whose mission was assisting mothers and small children could apply for a grant. Susan mentioned that there were a few others working with this population and we should call a meeting. A meeting was held with two ministers and a social worker.

The name of our group became The Minority Collaborative Task Force. An application was submitted to Family Council. However, because there were so many different partners and programs involved, it was not possible to have it funded the way we anticipated. Our desire was to have each program receive funding. After further discussion, Susan and I decided to work together on the project.

FROM MINORITY COLLABORATIVE TASK FORCE TO MINORITY DEVELOPMENT SERVICES OF STARK COUNTY (MDS)

The program was housed at my husband's church. We had two tables and one telephone with call waiting. The procedure for the Family Council Program, which, at that time was called Early Childhood Home Visiting (ECHV), was very tedious and required a tremendous amount of paperwork. I remembered what Susan had told me about paperwork, so I was willing to handle this part and Susan became the recruiter for staff and clients. FACES of Stark County became the Collaborative's fiscal agent.

After three months, Susan decided that she needed to spend more time with her agency. This left me as the remaining person in the collaborative. This was what I did not want, but this also showed me that God was still in control. He was taking me back to where He had originally wanted me when He told me I could not retire. Now, did I actually think I could outsmart God? Since it was no longer a collaborative effort, I changed the name of the agency to **Minority Development Services of Stark County (MDS)**, recruited board members and became a 501(c) 3 not-for-profit social service agency.

In a very short period of time, we had 100 plus clients in our caseload. This caseload included mothers with small children under the age of six. However, the majority of these mothers also had children over the age of six that needed services. I made several phone calls inquiring about potential funding and was told that a fairly new foundation, Sisters of Charity, might be interested.

MDS-SC agency logo

I made an appointment with the Executive Director. At the meeting we discussed MDS and my plans for the mothers and children involved in our program. It was a rather lengthy meeting with many questions for me to answer. I thought it was a good meeting and awaited a response regarding funding. Several weeks letter I received a letter denying funding. While I was hopeful that money would be granted, I was not disappointed. After all, I was new to Canton and had not established a relationship with anyone of significance.

I began to write proposals for equipment and was truly excited when my first $2,500 award was granted by the Ada C. and Helen J. Rank Charitable Trust. This allowed me to purchase a computer, software, and a few other needed items.

The grant received from Family Council was fee for service meaning we had to do the work, prepare a billing and then wait at least 15 days before we were reimbursed. I talked to the staff to see if they were willing to work until our billing was received. They all agreed. However, the billing took longer than anticipated. I was really perplexed on how to meet payroll until our reimbursement was received. I prayed and heard the Lord say, "Ask your husband!" Now, I heard this but thought I know He did not tell me to ask my husband for money to meet the agency payroll. Well, I kept praying and the voice said the same thing, "Ask your husband!"

Not waiting a third time for God's voice I went home and told my husband about the agency's financial situation. Without any hesitation, he said "How much do you need?" I said, "$2,500.00". He answered, "The church can make you a loan. When do you need it?" I just stared at him sort of in shock. He bucked his big eyes, stretched his neck forward and slowly repeated, "When do you need it?" I very quickly said, "Right away". He said, "No problem. You're not going to skip town are you?" and then he laughed. My husband has a wonderful sense of humor.

A short time later an announcement appeared in the newspaper stating the State of Ohio had an $18 million surplus of Temporary Assistance for Needy Family (TANF) funds. Our County (Stark) would receive a considerable amount of these funds. There were several informational meetings held and then the proposal process began. I submitted a proposal and MDS was blessed to receive $450,000.00.

Information regarding this funding was published in the paper and included the name of the funded agencies and the award amount. I received several phone calls asking how I was able to get this funding since I was "the new kid on the block!" I was told there were several others upset that MDS was funded. I just said, "Talk to my Father. He made this possible!" I remember Bishop T.D. Jakes preached a sermon that was titled "Favor Ain't Fair." I truly understand this after experiencing the favor of God.

This was the beginning stages of launching MDS. These additional funds gave us an opportunity to service the entire family. If we were not able to provide the services, referrals were made to agencies that could meet those needs. There are a lot of social service agencies in Stark County and the majority of them were very cooperative and willing to network.

With the additional funding I was able to hire several case managers, a bookkeeper, and a housing coordinator. With the addition of new staff, our client load continued to grow. With every new staff and client, there were new problems, longer working hours and no time for lunch.

Many of the mothers were in need of parenting classes. The majority of the mothers that contacted our office was 19-25 years of age and had as many as four children. As I spoke with these mothers it was very obvious that they needed parenting skills. I was informed that, at the time, the only available parenting classes were at Goodwill. It was also apparent that the majority of the mothers involved with the Department of Job and Family Services (DJFS) were African-American. I scheduled a meeting with DJFS to discuss the possibility of starting a parenting class for the African-American population. It took several meetings before DJFS gave me the green light to research curriculum for these classes.

I was able to locate a Black Parenting Class Program. However, in order to teach these classes, the instructor had to be certified. The closest certification program was in Chicago. One of the MDS staff traveled to Chicago and returned with the proper certification.

The client load continued to grow. Clients did not just live in the area where MDS was located but they came from throughout the County. MDS became recognized as a viable not-for-profit social service agency. I became involved in a lot of networking groups and made many presentations to funders explaining our mission and vision. Within a short period of time, 46% of our clientele were Caucasian. Because of this change in population, the MDS board made a decision that we should change the name of our agency. Minority Development Services of Stark County was no longer appropriate.

One of our board members, Bobby Fisher, thought we should use a name that had the same initials as our original name. After several weeks, the new name became **Multi-Development Services of Stark County.**

My search for new funding was an on-going process. I contacted City officials and anyone whose mission funded social service programs.

My research also led me to a group known as the "homeless collaborative." This was a group of directors and/or supervisors that had homeless shelter programs. I contacted the Executive Director of the YWCA who invited me to become a member of the collaborative. These agency representatives were very passionate and concerned about the lack of beds for the homeless population. During my third meeting and listening to one director after another talking about how many homeless people they had to turn away because there were no available beds, I talked to the Lord for guidance. He gave me the green light to open a homeless shelter. While working in Chicago, I was a department director overseeing a 150 bed homeless shelter.

My desire to open the shelter was expressed to several homeless shelter providers. They applauded my desire to do this but stated that funding was going to be very difficult to acquire. I appreciated their concern but knew that if I had a vision, the Lord would make provision and so I stepped out on faith. I had a great deal of experience working with this population while employed in Chicago.

Across the street from the MDS office was a house that looked as if it was ready to fall over. The siding was peeling off and it had no appeal for purchasing. However, my vision saw a beautiful home less shelter for families.

The members of my husband's church, Jesus Speaks Christian Center, and I stretched our hands toward that house and prayed that God would make it possible for MDS to purchase and use it as a homeless shelter.

I submitted a proposal to the Stark Community Foundation requesting funds to purchase the home. I remember talking to a kind lady named Cindy Lazor from the Foundation. She did not know me but believed in my vision for the Summit neighborhood. Cindy was able to convince her board to "take a chance" on me and supply the funding for this home. Faith has taught me that when God gives you a vision proceed as if what you see is already yours.

When contact was made to purchase the home, it had been sold. However, I did not become upset because I know that when God has something for you, you will receive it or something better. Members of Jesus Speaks continued to pray. Within three weeks, the house was back on the market and in two months, we owned the home. Look at God—what a wonderful **BLESSING!**

Shortly after the purchase of the home I called and made an appointment with Mayor Richard Watkins to introduce myself and discuss MDS' role in the neighborhood. When he learned that it was the Summit neighborhood he expressed concern and cautioned me that this was not a good area. He talked about the crime, drugs and prostitution. I then very assuredly expressed that this was the reason God placed me there.

At the conclusion of our meeting, I thanked him for his time and shook his hand. When I arose from my seat to leave he said, "Is there anything I can do for you?" I said, "Well I didn't come to ask you for anything but since you asked, my agency has a house that we recently purchased and are in need of funds for rehab." Mayor Watkins immediately picked up the telephone and told the person on the other end that he was sending me down to discuss a project.

After our discussion, the gentleman expressed that this was an exciting project. He said funds were available for rehab but a formal application had to be made. He then called in one of his staff who gave me all of the forms with instructions on how to proceed.

This next section I will show you how God blessed MDS with five (5) properties in one year.

The properties are as follows:

1001 7ᵗʰ St., NW (Purchased August 3, 2000—2,576 sq. ft. house) Families are Forever Shelter

618 Fulton Road, NW (purchased September 6, 2000—5,320 sq. ft.—Youth Services

714 Fulton Rd., NW—(Purchased August 1, 2000—4,180 sq. ft. house)—Transitional Housing

424 Fulton R., NW (THE FULTON HOUSE) (purchased October 2, 2000—9,555 sq. ft.) Administrative offices and special programs

414 Fulton (purchased October 23, 2000—7,211 sq. ft. house), house torn down and lot used for green space

(MDS' First Property) Families are Forever Shelter—1001 7th St., NW

Even though the Mayor's office gave me the information regarding possible funding for rehabbing the shelter, the proposal had to be approved by City Council. This was my first time applying for a rehab loan so I contacted Councilman Joe Hunter. He was very supportive and guided me through the process.

I was very excited when the letter arrived stating my proposal had been approved. I thanked the Councilman for his support and indicated I would keep him posted on the progress. Dave Roberts, my Housing Coordinator, and I met to review the next steps involved before the rehab work was to begin. We were required to acquire three contractor bids. This process took two months. This was a wonderful learning experience for me and information I would need for future projects.

Once we selected the contractor, Dave and I sat down to discuss the time frame and what, if anything, might slow down the process. I reflected back to a Chicago project involving contractors and how they gave me a deadline and it was five months after the deadline before the project was actually completed.

Another memory was watching contractors build my former church in Chicago, the Apostolic Church of God. Bishop was on the worksite everyday making sure that things were going according to plan. Whenever he and I would meet, he would hand me a hardhat and say, "Betty, let's go out on the site so I can show you what has been done." Bishop also told me that no matter how good a contractor is or once his deadlines have been set, it is important for you to monitor their work to keep them on tract. I remember all of those lessons about contractors not realizing that I would need this invaluable information.

Every day Dave and/or I were at the worksite even if it was for 10 or 15 minutes. Before the shelter was opened and the word spread that MDS was going to open a shelter for women and children, we received many calls from women asking when the shelter would be ready for occupancy.

The Families are Forever Shelter opened in 2001 with a ribbon cutting ceremony conducted by Mayor Watkins. The house was simply beautiful with carpeted floors, country kitchen, ruffled curtains at the windows and a children's play area in the lower level

Families are Forever Shelter—"before"

Families are Forever Shelter—"after"

After the Mayor toured the house he remarked, "Betty, I'm glad we partnered with you on this project and I hope we can do more." He then said, "This place is simply beautiful—a place where I could live." I jokingly said, "Mayor, if you ever become homeless, give me a call." We both had a good laugh.

It was exciting when our first family was enrolled. We conducted a thorough needs assessment to find out, other than being homeless, what programs and services were required to help her become self-sufficient. The orientation included a book with guidelines and rules. At Families are Forever, it was important that the mothers realized a program was connected to the bed(s) she needed.

The program included preparing a daily schedule that started from the time they were required to get out of bed at 7 a.m. to bedtime at 10 p.m. If not already working, they were required to look for employment, as well as enroll all school-aged children in the elementary school that was two blocks from the shelter. For those that had not completed their high school education, they were required to enroll in a General Educational Development (G.E.D.) class. Most of the mothers were receiving a welfare check and had an open case with the Department of Job and Family Services. Therefore, it was necessary for our staff to connect with the mother's worker. In conjunction with the MDS staff, the mothers would prepare a budget that was closely monitored.

The mothers were busy from early morning until bedtime. In order to fill their day, it was sometimes necessary to have them volunteer at the agency. Time on their hands often meant "trouble" such as re-connecting with an abusive spouse or boyfriend or hanging with friends that were involved in drug activity.

There was always a waiting list. Some mothers were living with relatives, friends or going from shelter to shelter. When our beds were full, the MDS case manager would contact other shelters for any available space. The last resort was asking the Salvation Army to give them a one night voucher to stay at a motel. The majority of our mothers were grateful for the opportunity that the shelter afforded them. Many received their GED, a few enrolled in college and, after leaving our shelter, all of them moved into their apartments.

The first year after the shelter opened, every month I received several telephone calls asking for information about opening a shelter. Most would start by saying "I have a house and want to make it a shelter for the homeless." Out of approximately 25 or 30 calls, one actually opened a shelter but it was in another county. Some called and thought it would be a good way to make money! It is my opinion that a shelter should never be started with the intent of "making money!" There is a lot of hard work that goes into making it comfortable, hiring the right staff and then providing necessary services for mothers and children.

The majority of funding that was available was not for staff but for operating the program. It was always difficult to get some of our funders to understand that you need staff to run programs and you can't continue to tax your current staff by adding to their responsibilities.

In addition to the City providing funding to rehab the house, we applied for and received City Emergency Shelter Grant funds to help with program expenses. However, there were no dollars for staff. In the beginning the administrative staff and I assisted our clients. A substantial amount of my time was spent working with the mothers and children. I worked 80 hours a week and many times without a paycheck. This is not uncommon in small social service agencies.

After four years of meetings and applying for funds from the Ohio Department of Development, we were awarded a grant for night staff.

Staff began to complain about the unwillingness of some of the clients to follow rules and keep the house clean. The referrals we received were for mothers that were discharged from other shelters. Against advice of staff there were some mothers we accepted because of the small children. However, in order to keep staff, we had to enforce our rules. This made it difficult to accept some of the referrals. There was a period of several months that the shelter was empty because of the referred mother's unwillingness to follow shelter rules. One of the mothers said to a staff person, "Your rules are too strict. I don't need a program I just want a place to sleep."

In 2003 my Leukemia patient hero, Lisa, and her friend Amy visited me. They wanted to experience living in a shelter and sharing with the homeless. They stayed at Families are Forever and had an opportunity to meet and interact with the family living there. They also had the privilege of serving the homeless at the Turn Around Outreach Center.

In 2008 a new Mayor was elected that brought in an entirely new team. I need to interject that we also had a new Councilman that was elected for his second term. As we did in past years, an application was sent to the city for an Emergency Shelter Grant. Much to my surprise and that of my board and staff, for the first time in eight years our application was denied!

When I inquired why our grant was not being awarded, I was told by the Community Development staff person that their research showed we had funding from other sources. This definitely was not true. The conversation between my office and the Mayor's Community Development staff went back and forth for about three weeks. The money they were referring to was connected with another one of our programs. Oops! They made a big mistake. However, it was too late to correct it.

This became a nightmare and many phone calls and a face-to-face meeting failed to resolve this dilemma. When I informed the staff person that I would then need to close the facility until we could secure funding, she said, "Then your shelter will be out of compliance and we (the city) will have to take it over!" Now that was really a blow to me. For the first time I experienced a lack of cooperation with the City. I didn't understand how the City could close a shelter when there were so many homeless people in Stark County!

I asked the representative what they were going to do with the money that was taken from our shelter and she replied, "We're going to use it in our office!" Now whether or not this was a true statement or something coming off the top of her head just to give me an answer, in my opinion, this was not a good way to spend Emergency Shelter Grant funds. Close a shelter and put it in the Mayor's budget? I did not go beyond this contact person to pursue whether or not this was a true statement. What I do know is that even when I explained that a mistake had been made and we did not have any other funding source, the City did not offer any alternative funding.

Needless to say, this was very disturbing and meant without these funds the MDS shelter would close. This was the topic of discussion at our board meeting. We all agreed that the next step should be to contact our Councilman. However, for a reason not made known to us, the Councilman for our Ward had withdrawn his support for our agency. Many attempts had been made to discuss the matter with him but there was no response. I was informed by several individuals in the Mayor's cabinet that the Councilman had told them NOT to give MDS any funds.

In a meeting with another member of the Mayor's staff, I was asked, "What kind of problem are you having with your Councilman?" My response was, "I really have no idea why all of a sudden he withdrew his support and would not even discuss it with me or the board. The problem started when the Weed and Seed Program was funded." The Mayor's representative then said, "I'm going to call a meeting with the two of you to see if we can work this out." I chuckled and said, "I'm positive the Councilman will refuse a meeting but please try." This meeting never happened.

At the time we were notified that new funding would not be available, we had a mother and two children in the shelter. We were able to move them into our transitional house until permanent housing was available. The other alternative to keeping the shelter open was to house a mother with small children who was either on welfare or employed. She would then be able to pay the utilities. Many of the women that we housed previously were welfare recipients and some of them were employed. We never asked them for any portion of their check. However, budgeting was strictly enforced.

Two months after transferring the family from our shelter to our transitional house, we received a call from a young mother with two small children in need of housing. The house she was living in had a fire that forced her to move. She received a monthly welfare check and was able to pay for the utilities. She was also attending college. She asked if we could extend her stay an additional 30 days at which time she and her children would be moving to Columbus, OH. The normal stay in a shelter is 90 days. We granted her request. At the end of the extension she informed us that everything was in place for her move to Columbus. She graciously thanked us.

The dialogue with the Mayor's office continued for another month with no resolve.

As of April, 2010, and the final year for the house to remain a shelter, the MDS Board will decide what they will do with the house since the agency owns it. When the city gives you government money to rehab a building/house for a shelter, it must remain a shelter for ten years.

MDS continues to seek funding from other sources and relies heavily on volunteers.

LIVING IN A FREE ENVIRONMENT (L.I.F.E.) AFTER SCHOOL YOUTH PROGRAM

According to the 2000 Census, the Summit neighborhood had 1,000 children between the ages of 5 and 18. There were no after school programs in the neighborhood, so the need was great.

I met with the school principal to discuss concerns for the children once school was dismissed. He agreed that an after-school program was needed and assured me he would be supportive if I was able to find funding.

A Cantonian informed me that funds might be available through the Alcohol and Drug Addiction Services Board (ADAS). The funds were referred to as Urban Minority Alcoholism & Drug Abuse Outreach Program ("UMADAOP").

After mentioning this to several persons I was told that the current Director of ADAS had commented that he did not want an UMADAOP in Canton. There were some racial overtones but I refused to let that stop me.

I made an appointment with the Executive Director, outlined my agency's mission and the need for an after school program in the Summit neighborhood. He was familiar with the drug infested neighborhood and began to discourage me. I was persistent and asked if there was any UMADAOP funding available. His answer was "There is some funding available but the deadline for applying is in two weeks. Also in order to apply, you must establish a board of which at least one person must be a credentialed drug abuse counselor." I told him I would get back to him in a few days.

Many calls were made to establish a board and find someone with the proper credentials. I was blessed to find someone that worked at Indian River Juvenile Correction Facility. She willingly agreed to serve on the board.

One week later with a list of board members, an outline for the after school program, and a budget, I met with the Director of ADAS. When I presented the information he looked at his Program Director and said, "Well, I guess we had better help her."

The application was completed and mailed to the Columbus office. The response from Columbus stated that there were no UMADAOP funds available for Stark County. These funds were administered by the Ohio Department of Alcoholism and Drug Addiction Services—ODADAS. However, there was another funding stream under "special services" and they awarded us $20,000.00.

The ADAS Board gave us an additional $18,000. 00. I was now in need of someone to coordinate the program.

Several weeks went by and I had not been able to find a Program Coordinator. I began to pray, continued my search and waited on the Lord to send the right person. Two weeks later I was introduced to a gentleman named Johnny Davis, a retired *American football running back* who played ten seasons in the *NFL* from (1978-1987).

Johnny had a love for gospel music and was an outstanding organist. He and I discussed the program. He shared with me his love for youth and his desire to work with this population. He also told me that he was looking for a program such as the one at MDS. His goal is to encourage young people to stay away from drugs and alcohol. We looked at one another and said, "Look at God."

During one of the LIFE sessions, I overheard some of the youth discussing how they would sell drugs to get money for "studio" time. Many youth, especially our young men, love to sing and rap. This conversation disturbed me so I interrupted and explained why this was not a good thing. They apologized and indicated the discussion was not meant for me to hear. I believe God intended for me to hear this. I immediately said, without even knowing what this meant, "I don't want you selling drugs; we'll open our own studio." The youth looked at one another and then me. One of them said, "Thank you Mrs. Smith, but that is something we don't think you can do" and then he chuckled. They did not realize that when you have a "vision" God makes "provision" and there is "nothing too hard for Him"!

I immediately began to write proposals and within a year our recording studio was up and running with state of the art equipment! We used the studio as a "carrot!" The youth had to study hard, have no failing grades, be obedient to their parent(s) and abide by the program rules before they would be able to use the studio.

During Johnny's 18 months with the program he was instrumental in starting a football camp that had guest appearances of some of the areas football greats such as Todd Blackledge, sports announcer for ESPN, and Garland Rivers, a Canton football player.

In 2004, Johnny invited me to partner with the Cleveland Clinic and several other programs in an anti-drug project.

Here are excerpts from a letter I received from Gregory B. Collins, M.D., Section Head, Alcohol & Drug Recovery Center Department of Psychiatry & Psychology, The Cleveland Clinic.

I'm writing today to let you know that our team of people involved in the video tape project with John Hay High School won several national awards for the final video tape production, which was entitled "It's All About Choices." We have not forgotten that you were a vital link in our chain in terms of developing the idea and being part of the final footage. As you remember, your section was shot at the Fulton House in Canton, Ohio with Johnny Davis and your kids.

The Telly Award which I'm including with this letter is basically a national award for an outstanding public service video production. It is somewhat akin to an Oscar or a Tony Award, and is given to very few productions out of thousands which are nominated every year.

Once again let me thank you for your outstanding contribution to this marvelous effort and please accept my sincere congratulations for an award well deserved. It's always a pleasure to work with you. I certainly value your personal friendship and support beyond measure.

During the second year of operation, I met with the Summit School Principal and asked if he would send a survey to parents of his students asking general sports and activity questions. He agreed. Two hundred forty-five out of 354 surveys were returned. The results indicated that if given the opportunity, the youth would love to learn the game of tennis, golf and how to swim. Very few of them were members of the Y or involved in any other kind of activity.

The following week I sent a press release to the newspaper asking for volunteers to work with the youth who wanted to learn tennis. I received calls from 16 individuals and 9 of them were able to make the time commitment. The volunteers ranged in age from 22 to 50.

In need of funding for equipment, I did an internet search and came in contact with the Midwest Tennis Association. After making contact by telephone and completing an application, we received a grant that allowed us to purchase tennis equipment. This contact put me in touch with the Northeast Ohio Tennis Association that also approved a grant.

The various grants from both of these associations allowed our youth to play tennis year round. In addition, a contact was made with Timken High School and Mr. Norman, the Tennis Coach assigned some of his students to work with our youth.

None of these youth had ever held a tennis racket or tennis ball. One of them remarked, "Ms. Betty, this is unbelievable that I'm actually learning how to play tennis. This is something I dreamed about." Now this made everything worthwhile.

In an effort to keep them motivated, I wanted something exciting for the youth. While internet searching for additional funding for tennis, I saw that Venus and Serena Williams were going to play against one another in

Cleveland. My fingers began to navigate through a lot of press releases until I found one with a contact for the game. I was able to get in touch with the person that was promoting the event, spoke with him, explained our program and within a few days received free tickets for 17 youth and 5 adults to attend the match between the Williams Sisters.

Not only were the youth excited but I was also. I was allowed to attend a pre-show event at the McDonald House. And to top that off I was also given back stage passes at one of the school events that allowed me to interview Venus and Serena for my Canton cable TV show. I also had my picture taken with them.

The L.I.F.E. Program is not only a safe haven for the youth, but also includes a homework center, computer lab, music, swimming, anti-drug curriculum, current events discussions, soccer, cheerleading, photography, yoga, and educational and recreational field trips. The youth also participate in parades in Canton, Akron and Cleveland.

Ms. Dottie Pressley, a former L.I.F.E. staff member and an outstanding gospel singer, recorded a DVD in our recording studio that sold at our local Bereans Christian Book Store. Proceeds from this DVD were donated to the L.I.F.E. Program.

As a part of our education and nutrition program, I thought it would be a plus if we had a garden. Across the street from our office were two vacant lots. I did a search and found the name of the person that owned the lots. After leaving several messages, I received a call. I gave the gentleman a brief explanation and history of MDS and the reason why I wanted to use the lots. He complimented me on the programs and then offered to sell them to me for what he owed on taxes. The amount owed was way out of reach for our small agency and, therefore, I immediately declined the offer. My next approach was to ask him to donate the lots. His counter offer was to allow us to use the lots for our garden. I accepted the offer.

After meeting with friends and some of our board members regarding the garden, I was given contact information for the Ohio State University Extension Program (OSUEP). This was a great contact that offered me information and an assigned person that would help establish our garden. This relationship resulted in the beginning and now five years of gardening. Each year we have three to five Master Gardeners working with our youth.

After being involved with the OSUEP for a year, I was asked to become one a member of their board which I accepted. These individuals educate our youth about gardening, from tilling the soil to harvesting. Many of our youth had never worked in a garden or eaten fresh vegetables such as green beans and zucchini. It was such a delight to watch the expressions on their faces as they witnessed a seed turn into something edible.

One very warm day after working in the garden one of the youth walked up to me, looked up with his big eyes sparkling, perspiration and dirt on his face and with a bit of a stutter he said, "Ms Betty, do you think I could have some seeds so my grandma can plant a garden? She told me when she was younger she used to have a garden."

I reached down and put my arms around him and said, "You pick out what you need and take them to your Grandma." He jumped up and down as he said, "Thank you Ms Betty, thank you." My heart just leaped for joy as tears trickled down my face thinking a few seeds could make a child so happy.

Every year the garden stops traffic, particularly when they see all of the youth busy working. In addition to the vegetables, there are herbs and beautiful flowers.

Mrs. Remel Moore joined our staff as the Youth Director. Her outstanding writing skills allowed us to receive many grants to carry on the work of MDS. She was also responsible for organizing our 4H Club, Girl Scout Troop, soccer team and other youth activities. Two MDS staff members have become Master Gardeners.

In 2008, the Summit Neighborhood Elementary School closed and the building became an Arts Academy. Because the neighborhood children were bused to two schools in other communities, it was necessary to transfer our after-school program to one of the schools.

In 10 years, the L.I.F.E. Program has served more than 750 youth between the ages of 6 and 13.

In addition to ADAS and ODADAS funding, we also received grants from the Stark Community Foundation, the Finish Line Foundation, Ohio Department of Education and others.

618 FULTON ROAD

After MDS had been in the 618 Fulton Rd. building a year, the landlord informed my husband that she no longer wanted to rent it and wanted to know if he was interested in purchasing. My husband responded that it was too small for the church to purchase, but encouraged her to talk to me because of the programs I had established in the building.

The owner was a very kind, elderly lady and stated she would give me three or four months to see if I could get funding to purchase the building. The proposal was written to the Hoover Foundation. While waiting for funding, our programs continued. We were now into our third month and in need of a miracle to purchase the building. I was calm knowing that if it is for us to purchase the building, funding would be made available.

In the fourth month, I was busy working on our annual Golden Dove Awards and received a call from the Executive Director of the Hoover Foundation. He informed me that the foundation was going to award MDS a grant to purchase and rehab the 618 Fulton Road building. I had to contain myself to keep from crying. In my heart I was saying "Thank you Jesus." I graciously thanked him. Within a month we received the check.

MDS became the owner and rented space to Jesus Speaks Christian Center. We had this arrangement for several years until Jesus Speaks purchased a building at 1103 McKinley, N.W. The church is still in the Summit neighborhood.

Our client numbers continued to grow but the staff remained the same. The hardest thing for me to do was refuse someone service. A good thing was there were other social service agencies and we were able to make referrals. The majority of the agencies were very good at collaborating but, as with anything else, there were some not as receptive.

I remember one evening while sitting at home my mind was filled with programs, clients, funding, etc. My faith was beginning to weaken. I prayed and asked God to send me something that would assure me that He was still guiding me and I was doing what He desired.

The next day while sitting in my office a young lady, whose clothes were somewhat dirty and torn, walked into the office and said, "Miss, I have something I must give you, please take it." She opened her hand and in it were two crinkled and some-what dirty one-hundred dollar bills.

I said, "Thank you very much but I can't take this from you." I was looking at the way she was dressed and assumed she could not afford to make this donation.

She then said, "I have paced up and down the sidewalk outside your building for the past 20 minutes not really wanting to come in and give you this money but something or someone spoke to me and said, Go inside and give it to her. So please take this and I will feel so much better".

I took the money and began to write a receipt. She walked toward the door and said, "No, please do not give me a receipt. I just obeyed what I knew I had to do." She left. I immediately knew that God had sent me an angel as a sign that I should continue my work. There have been other times in my life when I needed a sign from God and He always sent it. Don't knock it if you haven't tried it.

The MDS Programs, that were located at 618 Fulton Road, were "busting out at the seams". There was not enough room for staff or youth. We ran out of chairs which meant some of the youth had to sit on the floor. This was a good problem to have. The staff and I were pleased that the parents recognized our facility as a "safe haven" for their children. What we didn't want to do was turn youth away knowing there was not another program available in the neighborhood.

424 FULTON ROAD—THE FULTON HOUSE

Several months after the shelter opened I received a call regarding the availability of a two-story frame house with 3 bedrooms, 2 baths, living room, dining room, kitchen, enclosed porch and unfinished basement. It was located on the corner of 5th and Fulton, one block from our current office. The owner indicated that he no longer lived in Canton nor did he want the house. He said to me that someone informed him about the work I was doing with families and the house would be an opportunity to expand our programs. This was a Section 8 house and currently occupied. The owner made it clear that once the house was sold, the family would be relocated.

After touring the house, I told him that MDS did not have funds or any use for the property. We shook hands; I thanked him and returned to my office.

Several days later I received a call from the owner of the house once again trying to convince me to purchase it. I repeated what I had previously stated that we had no funding or use for the building.

Three months later this same gentleman walked into my office at 618 Fulton Road, placed the keys on my desk and said, "I really want you to have this house. We can figure out how you pay for it later." He then walked away.

I said "Lord, now what?" Immediately the Lord showed me the many programs that could be established in the house and how it could be of service to the community. I became excited.

This house, located at 424 Fulton Road, two blocks from our office, later became known as the **Fulton House**. It was in a residential zone and because we would be offering programs and no one would be living there, it would now be referred to as commercial property. This meant it would be necessary to go through a zoning change. Now did I know anything about zoning? Of course not, but God had people in place to assist. If He takes you to it, He will lead you through it.

I immediately called a meeting with my Housing Director to discuss the house and possibilities for its use. It was agreed that it would allow us to expand our programs. Of course, the concern was whether or not we would be able to get funding. I told him that I knew God was in the plan and would work things out.

The first order of business was to hire an architect and contractor. A meeting with the Building Code Department was a must. Now that was an experience! There were many meetings with the architect, contractor, code department and sub-contractors. In an effort to move the project along, I had to make many, many phone calls, establish new contacts, and be available based on everyone else's schedule. In the meantime, I was waiting for a response from several foundations that would provide necessary funds.

During this process, I met a lot of wonderful people and some "not so" wonderful people. There are always those that drag their feet or seemingly deliberately make things difficult. However, you must persevere. The Bible says that tests and trials come to make us strong! So true! When you only have a few staff, you MUST wear many hats, have a flexible schedule and be able to "turn on a dime"!

I soon discovered a zoning change was already in the works for another project in the area and MDS could be added. While we're trying to figure it out, God has already worked it out!

During the course of meetings, phone calls and other necessary business items, I received a letter from the Timken Foundation awarding us a grant for this project.

The contractor that was selected for this project had some personal problems and informed me that he would not be able to do the work. However, he recommended someone that he felt would do a good job. Well, this definitely was not the case. Dave and I were busy with other projects and programs and did not have time to adequately supervise the contractor. The contractor took advantage of this and failed to ask for my input on selecting bathroom or kitchen appliances or light fixtures. It was my opinion that the contractor saw that I was a woman and probably did not have a lot of knowledge about rehab. He was wrong!

Before the rehab project with our shelter, I had experience working with contractors in Chicago in a complete renovation of my condo. This work was similar to the MDS shelter project that required new floors, walls, windows, etc. I forgot to mention that when the contractor who worked on the 1001 7th Street shelter put on a sub-standard roof and thought he was going to get by, I insisted it be removed and replaced with one of better quality. Well, he was honest and admitted that it was not up to par and he had used some neighborhood men to "throw it" up. He put on a new roof.

The funding received was only enough to complete the first floor. I still had the basement and second floor that needed to be completed.

I hired the same contractor that rehabbed the 1001 7th St. Shelter. After he was honest with me about the shelter roof and put on a new one, I had a trust level with him that made it easy for me to hire him to rehab the 424 house.

Without any available funding, I stepped out on faith and asked the contractor to begin working on 424.

My staff thought I had really gone a bit too far with my faith. I told them that God honors faith and He hasn't failed me yet.

The basement at 424 was a disaster zone with lots of hanging wires, dirty brick walls, a floor that had broken pieces of cement in every room, an old fashioned sink that did not work and no windows.

The shelter that was recently rehabbed had to be completely gutted because of its poor condition and the contractor worked miracles with this facility so I knew he would be able to do the same with 424.

In the meantime, I wrote several grants asking for funds to complete the project. My prayer was, "Dear God, please send money before the contractor needs to be paid."

Dave and I closely monitored the contractors work and were pleased with the process. The contractor made a lot of great suggestions about the basement and second floor.

I told him I always wanted an office with a lot of windows so he took out the very tiny windows and put in a 8 by 4 1/2 window that allowed me to overlook Fulton Road. I could actually see an entire block from my window. This later proved to be very good as it allowed me to witness prostitutes soliciting cars. Whenever I was in my office looking out the window and would see a prostitute, I would pick up the telephone, dial the number and within minutes the police were present. I was also able to watch the children get off the school bus and happily walked to the 618 building for their after-school program.

Let me digress and share with you a short story. One day while I was looking out my large office window, I saw a prostitute standing on the corner. I walked down the stairs, out the door, down the street and talked with the very attractive, tiny, and blond-haired lady. She was very nervous and began to walk away. I told her not to be afraid I just wanted to talk to her. She shared with me that she was a prostitute because it was the only way she could take care of her children. She had a drug felony and no one would hire her. I gave her information about the agency, some possible job leads and told her to stay in touch with me. I continued by saying, "Perhaps after I become more established in the agency, I might be able to hire you." She looked at me with water welling up in her eyes, a puzzled look on her face and said, "Would you really hire me?" I said, "Yes, if I had a job that I thought you could do." She thanked me and walked away.

I have many stories like this about prostitutes, homeless, alcoholics, drug addicts, etc. Many people with these problems just need for someone to care. But for the Grace of God, it could be any one of us. I like the song that says, "Reach out and touch somebody's hand, make this world a better place if you can." That's what MDS is all about.

Back to the 424 story. I picked out very vibrant colors of green and yellow for the basement. It was simply amazing how the basement was transformed into beautiful offices for the staff.

It was actually the day the contractors completed their work that I received three checks in the mail from foundations. The amount was exactly what I needed and nothing left over! This made true believers out of some of the staff and increased my faith!

The Fulton House became the administrative building and housed our information and referral department, food pantry, and parenting classes. It also became a "safe haven" for our seniors.

Within 25 feet of 424 Fulton was a large house that had been boarded up for approximately five years. There was a lot of drug activity so it became necessary for me to pray about funds to purchase the facility. I had an architect and the Preservation Society tour the facility to see if it was worth fixing, but was informed it would be best to have it torn down. Once again, **God blessed** with the funding and we were able to get it razed. This lot is used as green space. The youth in our SNET II program, which you will learn more about in a later chapter, and the maintenance staff keep it well manicured.

1002 TEN-UNIT APARTMENT BUILDING FOR MOTHERS AND CHILDREN (Rental property—2002-2006)

While the 424 project was being renovated, I received a visit from a prominent Canton businessman. He expressed that he was very impressed with the shelter MDS renovated and the type of program we had established. He said, "Betty, I have a ten-unit apartment building for rent and perhaps you can use it for the families you serve. If you would like to see it, I can arrange for someone to pick you up and give you a tour of the building." I agreed.

Later that afternoon I was walking through the ten-unit apartment building and "saw potential!" There was quite a bit of work that needed to be done but I knew there were a lot of mothers with small children that needed a place to live. Knowing this was a good thing for our families and God would supply every need, I agreed to use the building! Another plus to the building is that it was on a huge lot (2.3 acres) that we could utilize as long as we kept the lawn mowed.

This house that we refer to as "1002" had its problems, but nothing too hard for God. My faithful and committed Housing Director, Dave, became the person that I would rely on to make sure that things were in order. We put together a grant that was funded through the Homeless Coalition. We were one of the first new agencies funded through the Coalition in more than ten years. This grant paid for all staff, including maintenance and security. It also provided funds to subsidize rent for mothers that had little or no income.

1002 was always full with a waiting list. One of our rules was that no men were allowed in the house unless it was the father of the child(ren). Well, you can imagine how hard that was to monitor. We were located not far from a drug district, so that in itself was challenging. In spite of the problems, we had success stories and provided meaningful services for those mothers that chose to follow the program.

During our fifth year, we had a major increase in utilities and a need for another staff person. We requested additional funding from our grantee. However, this particular year the Federal Government decreased funding for most grantees and asked that we operate programs with the same dollars as in the previous year. This was simply impossible so we had no choice but to gradually phase out the program.

Funding is always a challenge for social service agencies and particularly small ones like MDS. Most government grants are fee for service. You perform the service and then you are reimbursed. It is, therefore, necessary to have operating funds.

Most foundations and other funding sources will not give you operating dollars making it imperative to have fundraisers or necessary to solicit for unrestricted dollars

My Board and I had hoped by this time we would have been eligible for United Way funding. For one year we received a Community Initiative Grant but soon thereafter this program was discontinued. We had numerous meetings, made presentations and as of 2010 have yet to receive any UW funding.

In 2005, once again our bank account was down to its last dollars. I prayed and asked God for an answer. You never know who God will send to answer your prayers so don't be surprised. I met with a very well-known and respected businessman in Canton and told him about my financial dilemma. He asked that I call several board members together to discuss the situation.

He also said, "Betty, MDS is an anchor in this community and the work you are doing must continue. We will figure out a way to get you through this crisis." I shook my head and said, "Thank you God."

The following week we met with the board president and two additional board members. Our discussion focused on programs, staffing, and budgets. At the end of the discussion, the businessman that asked me to call the meeting took out his personal check book and wrote a check for $30,000.00. He said, "This is a loan, pay me back when you can." Tears welled up in my eyes as I said, "Thank you and God bless you." This person later informed the board president that we did not need to repay the loan. What a **Blessing in the Midst of my Pain!**

714 FULTON ROAD—TRANSITIONAL HOUSING

The maximum stay in our shelter was 90 days. In most cases, this was not enough time to provide services that would enable our mothers to make substantial lifestyle changes. Canton had only a few transitional housing beds or a facility that will allow the client to stay up to two years.

One sunny afternoon, Councilman Hunter stopped by my office and informed me that a very nice house, a half block from our 618 Fulton Road facility, had been sitting empty for eight years. He thought I should see if there was any possibility of acquiring it to use for our mothers and children.

I immediately walked down the street to look at the outside of the house. It was a newly-sided gray, two-story house with a porch that was in need of repair and what appeared to be new windows. I thought, "This house has a lot of possibility." I met with Dave Roberts and asked that he locate the owner. After some research, he made contact and set up a meeting. The owner was a very nice elderly gentleman who was quite happy to meet with us. He said that his wife was bugging him to get rid of the house. The owner told us that he had started rehabbing it himself, but it was a very slow process. He also said that four years ago he put on new siding and a new roof.

714 Fulton Road—Transitional Housing

The inside of the house had hard-wood floors, beautiful dark mahogany wood, 1 bedroom, full bath, large foyer, living room, dining room and kitchen downstairs. Upstairs was 2 bedrooms, a sitting room and a full bath in the front part and a half bath and two additional rooms in the back portion. There was also another set of stairs leading down to the outside of the house. In addition there was a full attic that could be used for storage.

We were able to negotiate a great price for the house and acquired funding from another local foundation for the purchase.

We were in perfect timing to apply for a grant through our local Homeless Coalition that would provide funding for rehab and staff for families in transition.

I want to share a story with you about this house that is very interesting and caught the attention of many people, including the media!

714 Fulton Road became known as the **HAUNTED HOUSE!**

During the rehab process of 714, one day while busy at work in my office, the head contractor knocked on my door. When I opened it, standing before me was a very frightened man with eyes as big as saucers and skin white as a sheet. I did not even get an opportunity to ask him anything before he said, "Mrs. Smith there is someone other than my workers in 714." Of course I had to ask several questions before he told me that he thought there was a "ghost" living there.

I began to chuckle, but he was not laughing. I then asked him to explain why he made this statement. His reply was "One of the doors keeps slamming. The workers said they felt like someone was standing over them and things were being moved without any of the workers moving them." He then asked me to come down to the house and I obliged. He showed me where he had placed some of his tools and where he later found them, which is not where he originally had placed them. He said something else very strange. One day he walked into the house and it was quite cold. He asked one of the workers if any of them had turned on the air conditioning. The worker replied, "We haven't installed the unit yet." He then said to me, "That is another sign that a ghost is present; I'm told it is always cold when they are around!" We chatted for a few more minutes and I was able to convince him to continue to work, but this didn't last long.

Several days later the next visit was from one of the workers. He said that while outside working on the handicap ramp he glanced up and saw an elderly lady with pretty curly white hair standing in the window. He thought I was giving someone a tour until he tried to go inside the house and discovered the door was locked and my car was not outside. He then said, "Mrs. Smith we can't work in there any longer, you definitely have a GHOST."

The real convincing ghost story came the next day when the contractor called and asked me to come to the building. When I arrived, he was standing outside and gazing up at the windows. I asked, who opened all of the windows? He said, "That's what I called to ask you." He said, "The strange thing is all of the windows were raised 7 and ¼ inches; I measured all of them. (The address is 714.)

He further commented that he and one of his workers had moved a very heavy door on the second floor into one of the bedrooms. Someone took the door out of the bedroom and placed it in front of the room where the old lady with the white hair was standing. Also in front of the room was a stack of paint cans with sticks on the top. The real frightening thing was this door was so heavy it took two men to move it! How could a little ole lady move it! After they noticed the door being moved and the paint cans, the lights began to flicker and he ran out of the house!

Well, the story soon spread and we were swamped with reporters from newspapers and television stations as well as many curious people riding by and pointing at the house. We had a major traffic jam.

The "Ghost" story made the front page of the Local section in our newspaper, The *Repository.*

I remember receiving a call from one of the television stations that was really curious and wanted some kind of evidence that we had a ghost. When they arrived at the house I said, "Well, let me see if I can give you some kind of proof." By this time we had named our ghost Matilda. I said, "Matilda we have some reporters here that do not believe you exist." I then pointed to a crack in the floor that led to the basement. I continued talking to Matilda and said, "The light in the basement is out. We are going outside for a few minutes and while we're gone, please turn on the light." We went outside and two minutes later returned to discover the light in the basement was "on"! Well, the cameraman almost dropped his camera. What a story! This story ran for a week and our phones were jumping off the hook.

We had so much publicity that I came up with an idea to make some money for our food pantry. It was Halloween time—yes, you guessed it. I had an open house, charged $5 per person. We made quite a bit of money. I was so amazed that there are so many people that "ghost chase." I was led to websites that had all kinds of information about ghosts, received a lot of letters, and many people wanted to talk to me about the house.

Several reporters from our local paper, *The Repository,* asked if they could spend the night! I agreed. When I spoke to one of them the next day, she explained that there was nothing out of the ordinary that happened except she was not able to get any photos. The only thing that showed was a "bright" light! This photo was printed in the paper. I remember during the Halloween showing that several photographers commented that they knew there was a ghost in the house because they were unable to take pictures. The shutter would spin out of control!

During the course of all the publicity, I had several families contact me that had lived in the house. One of them asked if they could come by just to reminisce. I agreed and they brought their entire family along with photo albums. One interesting part of the visit was when we went to the basement one of the ladies walked behind a wall and showed them a hidden room. She commented that this is where she used to hide when she wanted to get away! One of her sisters said, "I always wondered where you went." They all had a big laugh. I was unaware of this space. It was well hidden.

Another young lady contacted me and asked to come by the house. She had also lived there. She told me a story about an old lady that resembled the one who the gentleman described he had seen in the window on the second floor. She said, "The lady that lived here loved this house and often talked about how she never wanted to leave. However, when she was up in age she did move away. She has since died."

A few weeks after the ghost story hit the paper, I received a very important phone call. The voice on the other end said, "I would like to move the lady on that is trapped in your house at 714 Fulton Road." She further said, "If you will allow me to stay overnight I'll get rid of your ghost." I agreed! After the night's stay, she said, "You have two ghosts—a lady and a gentleman and I will need to stay another night." Once again I agreed. She said I will take some blessed oil and my Bible with me.

The next day she called and said, "They are now gone!" I did not ask any questions. I called my contractor and told him what had happened and he said he would see if the crew would go back to work. They agreed and we have not heard anymore about ghosts.

We still have people asking about the "ghost house!" For you non-believers and yes I was one until I actually witnessed some of these events and others such as the lights flickering and doors slamming, do you have an explanation for these happenings? I sure do not!

When it was time to move a family into the 714 house, I asked the mother if she was afraid of ghosts, then I chuckled. She said, "Mrs. Smith, I'm not afraid of ghosts, I have the Lord on my side and my family and I need a place to stay!" They moved in the following week.

This family stayed the entire two years. While living at 714 she received her G.E.D. and enrolled in one of our two-year colleges. At the end of her two years, she and her four children moved into their own home.

Transitional housing, just like our shelter, had its share of challenges. We had some mothers that did not want to follow a program. They just wanted a place to live without any structure. This was not permissible. Our program guidelines specifically spelled out that mothers had to be in school, work or both. They had to have a plan for what their children would be doing on a daily basis and if they had an income, a portion of it had to be saved.

In 2000, MDS purchased five properties. This was definitely God's plan for the agency. There is no way I could have accomplished this without God. *When God gives you vision, move forward. He promised to supply our every need according to His riches in glory!*

There was a lot of work involved, many challenges and some pain but in **the midst of it, God BLESSED!**

SUMMIT NEIGHBORHOOD ENRICHMENT TEAM (SNET)

In 2000, the Summit neighborhood was identified as a portion of the city with long-standing issues that have contributed to the decline of property appearances and values and the loss of a sense of pride and self-esteem. Ninety-four percent of the 458 children that attended the Summit Elementary School were eligible for the free lunch program. Summit had a population of 4,564 and 60% of the homes housed single parents. Summit had one of the highest incidents of drugs, alcohol and prostitution in the city and was 65% renter occupied.

Because of the above demographics and concerns, Mayor Watkins agreed to allow me and one of my staff, Dave, to meet with Safety Director Blair and his staff to discuss the possibility of forming a team that would walk through the neighborhood. The purpose was to take monthly walks throughout the neighborhood and identify vacant houses, building and/or health code violations, junk cars or cars with improper licenses on the streets or on properties, and make sure there were no small children left alone.

Our first meeting was held at the Summit Elementary School. The room was filled with enthusiastic and energetic men and women. We were all on the same page and our goal was to make the Summit neighborhood a better place in which to live. At this meeting, Councilman James (not his real name) suggested I be the spokesperson. The recommendation was unanimously accepted. We then decided that the name of the group would be called the Summit Neighborhood Enrichment Team (SNET).

Members of SNET consisted of MDS staff, various City of Canton officials from the Health, Building Code, and Police Departments, the City Safety Director, and several local Canton City Council representatives. Others included representatives from Summit School, Summit United Neighbors, Hammer and Nails, Landlord and Tenant's Association, and a representative from the Stark County Department of Job and Family Services

As a result of our first year's walk through the neighborhood, we were able to identify 400 boarded up houses and 116 houses that had code violations. It was great to partner with this team because they had access to owner information.

The monthly SNET meetings were exciting and very engaging. It provided me and my staff an opportunity to interact with others that were interested in making the Summit neighborhood a better place to live.

During one of our walks, I was talking with the Councilman about other MDS programs and services and asked if he would be interested in serving on the board. He readily agreed. I told him I would discuss it with the board and someone would contact him.

Abandoned house

At the next board meeting, it was unanimously decided that the Councilman would be added to our list. In addition to the Councilman, the board chair had two additional members that were added, one was an attorney and the other a member of the Canton City Schools Board of Education.

In addition to walking the neighborhood every month, MDS staff would send letters to owners of boarded up houses in an effort to find out their intentions for the property. In the letter, the owner is asked if he/she no longer wanted the property, would they consider deeding it to MDS.

One of the owners responded, met with Dave and me, and told us they no longer wanted the property and would like to donate it to MDS. We graciously accepted, had it assessed, and was told it would take $75,000 plus to rehab. This property, **601 Fulton Road, N.W.**, (Date of transaction, 9-8-2008, 3555 sq. feet) is two doors from our community garden. We have attempted to get the City to raze it for us, but were told there currently are no funds available. Once it is razed, we will use it for green space.

Our neighborhood SNET walks became so popular that other groups decided to do the same. It was very interesting that no matter who did the walks or what neighborhood, folks referred to them as SNET walks. Remember, the S in SNET stands for Summit, the neighborhood where MDS is located.

Periodically, Mayor Creighton would accompany us on our walks. She saw the benefit and called to inform me that she was going to do a similar walk but would include some of the faith-based community and more of the streets and sanitation department members. I thought this was a good idea. The day after her first walk, someone called and said, "I thought you need to know that the Mayor took a group of people on a SNET walk." I let them know that I was aware of the walk and thanked them for calling. After I hung up the phone I chuckled.

Mayor Creighton was very supportive of MDS and always available when needed. She was the kind of Mayor that was a phone call or e-mail away.

Ten years later the SNET team continues their walks. There are less than 200 boarded up houses. We have a new school that originally was the Summit Elementary School but because of many changes in the school system and budget cuts, it is now the Arts Academy of Summit. There are new market rate houses that were built across from the Arts Academy and many of the boarded up houses have either been torn down or purchased and renovated. Some of these houses have been sold and others are rental properties.

SNET II

In the fall of 2007, MDS launched SNET II, a unique collective of youth who live in the neighborhood, adults, community activists, government servants, businesses and associations, who began to clean up and continue to transform the Summit neighborhood. Even though the SNET program is successful in meeting its goals, there are still problems with abandoned properties. Many attempts are made to contact owners of these abandoned properties but most are unsuccessful.

The major focus and goal of SNET II is to rid the Summit neighborhood of the substantial amount of blight and related conditions in a designated area that has been brought on by slum landlords and vacant and abandoned houses.

The neighborhood has been divided into four quadrants with the goal to partner with residents to keep lawns mowed, trash placed in containers, and just be neighborly.

The first task was to prepare proposals requesting funding for the project. One of my staff, Mrs. Moore, asked for my vision and then began to put everything on paper. She wrote an excellent program with graphics and statistics. It was then up to me to present the proposal to potential funders.

I compiled a list of past, current and hopefully new funders. Before mailing the proposal, I called Cindy from the Stark Community Foundation and asked for a meeting. We discussed the proposal and the positive impact it could have on the neighborhood and the City. Cindy was excited about the idea of using youth that lived in the neighborhood. However, she thought the budget was too high and asked that I review and make adjustments. The original budget was in excess of $200,000 that included stipends for the youth, staff, beautification material such as flowers, seeds, mulch, hanging baskets, etc. and tools such as rakes, weed whackers, lawn mowers, shovels, gloves, etc. Start up materials and tools were very costly. I made some budget adjustments, scaled the program back so the bottom line was under $175,000.00.

Cindy then arranged for me to meet with several foundations. After hearing my presentation and passion for the program, they were on board to provide some of the funding. Within six months, we had three-fourths of funds needed for the program.

Once funding was secured, Dave and I met with one of the staff at Timken High School, explained the program and asked if a meeting could be arranged to speak with students that lived in the Summit Neighborhood. The teacher was excited and within the next few weeks a meeting was held with 30 students.

I gave the group an over-all orientation of MDS and the SNET II Program. After the presentation, I asked that if any of the students were interested in working in the program, they should remain for a group interview that would be followed by one-on-one interviews. Twenty-two of the 30 remained. Out of the 22, we hired 12 of the youth.

All of the youth admitted that while they wanted to improve the neighborhood where they live, they really needed the stipend that went along with the job. Some had responsibilities to help pay bills, assist with taking care of their younger siblings or buying clothes for school.

Two of the young ladies had children. One had a two-year-old and one on the way. Another was pregnant with her first child. I was not aware of the new pregnancies until they had been in the program for two months. They felt comfortable enough to discuss their situation and asked not to be terminated. The staff was instructed to find research or other clerical assignments that were inside the building. Both of them had clerical skills and proved to be very valuable in assisting with paperwork and telephone calls for the SNET II program.

SNET II has proven to be a very viable program for the neighborhood. One of Stark County's mega churches, Rivertree, was very supportive of this project. One of their Youth Pastors, Jason Lantz, led the charge to begin recruiting volunteers from Malone College, now University. Jason spoke to his Pastor about the work that MDS was doing in the Summit neighborhood and invited me to make a presentation at two of their Sunday morning worship services. At this meeting, I shared the story about how God assigned me to establish MDS in the Summit neighborhood. I also shared information about SNET II and how the youth are now a part of the solution and not the problem. The congregation was very receptive and some of them volunteered to help with the monthly clean up project.

Our biggest support for the monthly clean up sessions is students from Malone University. The faithful and dedicated leaders as of December, 2009 are Eddie Herrera, Jared Adams and Nick Battilana. These Christian young people arrive at 8:30 a.m. one Saturday every month. They come in the sun, rain or snow, full of energy and singing God's praises as they prepare to clean dirty lots, rake and mow lawns, bag debris and sometimes remove dead animals. These youth, along with our SNET II youth, are beautifying and revitalizing the neighborhood.

The SNET II youth are given a small stipend, of which a portion must be placed in a savings account. In addition to working to beautify the neighborhood, this program teaches them how to become a better neighbor, provides them with necessary tools for building self-esteem, budgeting, dealing with peer pressure, and tutoring. Many times the seniors, who were once afraid of this group of young people, now call the office and ask for their help with yard work.

In addition to mowing lawns and picking up debris, the youth, under the supervision of Dave and me, map the entire area. This includes color coding abandoned houses, empty lots, owner occupied homes, and rental properties. Lastly, local artists paint beautiful art work on the boarded up houses. Our first project for painting boards took place in our Arts District in Downtown Canton. We were able to utilize one of the empty warehouse buildings for our painting project. The First Friday in June the SNET II youth put artwork on seven boards that would fit over the doors and windows of some of the abandoned houses.

It was during this project that several youth discovered they actually had artistic skills. One of the young ladies drew a crowd as she patiently, and with a stroke of an artist's brush, drew curtains around a window and painted a flower pot that sat on a window sill. She was so involved in her work that she had not noticed the crowd that had gathered around to watch her paint. After she put the final touch on the flower pot, she took her hand, wiped her brow as she smudged paint on her face. She looked up and smiled as she noticed the people.

Artwork on boarded house 1

MDS youth drum line

Our biggest painting project was organized by Todd Walburn and Brennis Booth, owners of 2nd April Art Galarie. We had 50 plus artists of all ages that made one of the worse looking blocks in the neighborhood come alive with bright colors and pictures of hope! It's amazing what some artwork and mowed lawns can do for a neighborhood that has been devastated previously.

Every year our local United Way has a Day of Caring. The past several years we have been blessed to have up to 50 volunteers assist in beautifying the neighborhood. One group helped tear out old carpeting, put in a new floor and lay new carpeting at our youth center.

Many of the clean ups are supported by John Stone a local photographer who captures the workers as they revitalize the community. He puts the wonderful photos to music and shares this awesome day with you tube viewers. At the end of one of our clean up sessions, Elec Simon from the Broadway production of STOMP and a summer employee of MDS, picked up his drum sticks and began to beat on garbage cans, paint cans, yard tools and anything else he could find that would make a sound and keep the rhythm flowing. The workers, with pizza and beverages in hand, gathered around to watch Elec display his awesome talent with just two sticks and anything available that would clang. They were mesmerized!

Whenever our SNET II youth mow a lawn, clean up debris, etc., they leave a sign in the yard indicating that SNET II of MDS had taken care of the property. As a result of one of the signs being in a yard at **804—8th Street, N.W.**, I received a call from the owner. He was a minister and lived in New York. From our conversation, I learned that he was in a wheelchair and was doing similar social work in New York as MDS was doing in Canton.

He was also an investor and had never seen the property in Canton. His plan was to sell the 8th Street property on EBay. The property has a double lot and a seven-room house for a total of 4,620 sq. ft. Several phone calls later, he said that if I wanted to purchase the lots and house, he would sell all of it for $4,000. I was able to get a donor to purchase the property. The property was too costly to rehab so we asked the City if they would demolish it for us. Because of budgeting problems, the City indicated that, at this time, they would not be able to tear it down.

Tire garden

I was able to recruit a group of volunteers to plant a beautiful tire garden on the lot.

The neighbors around this property were so pleased that we purchased the house and land; they said they would make sure no one bothered the tire garden because it was the most beautiful thing on the block.

It would be impossible to manage the seven (7) MDS properties without the loyal and dedicated maintenance staff, Dan Byrd, Brennis Booth, Sr., and Sam Settles. God truly sent them to MDS.

WEED AND SEED (W & S)

During the 10 years of working at MDS, The W & S Program was my most challenging. This is one government program that I really felt had potential to help restore safety and bring harmony to neighborhoods such as Summit. However, egos and politics got in the way. I learned a great deal and am sure the experiences will be useful in another one of my life's journeys. God did not say that life would be easy.

Weed and Seed is a five-year, multi-agency strategy administered through the U.S. Department of Justice. The strategy involves a two-pronged approach: A community-oriented policing component bridges weeding and seeding strategies. Officers obtain helpful information from area residents for weeding efforts while they aid residents in obtaining information about community revitalization and seeding resources.

The W & S project was brought to the attention of the Summit Neighborhood Enrichment Team (S.N.E.T.), a program that is mentioned in an earlier chapter, during one of our monthly walks in the neighborhood. The young lady that had information about W & S was involved in the program in Akron OH that is less than 30 minutes from Canton. She was impressed with our S.N.E.T. walks and indicated that the W & S Program would provide funding to help in our efforts to revitalize the neighborhood.

In an effort to gather more information about W & S, Dave Roberts and I visited with the Safe Haven Director in Akron. She gave us a tour and shared valuable information about how the safe haven was operated. It was refreshing to know that the MDS's after school project qualified as a "safe haven" and already had many of the programs that were required. She did caution us that it was very important to chose the right fiscal agent and make sure that everyone involved is in tune and on the same page as it relates to revitalizing the neighborhood. She shared some difficulties they had experienced in Akron as a result of everyone not having the same agenda as it related to programs, fiscal responsibility and over-all leadership.

The Canton W & S process involved numerous meetings before the first application was submitted. The Steering Committee consisted of various businesses, social service agencies and city officials. There were also a few residents. When the meetings were first scheduled, I was not extended an invitation. It was after the second meeting that one of the members asked why I had not been attending. I relayed that I was not aware of the meetings. He then suggested that I attend the next meeting since MDS programs were being discussed as being a plus for the W & S grant process. He added, "However, MDS name was not mentioned." The member further stated that those familiar with the Summit neighborhood and MDS were very much aware that the programs mentioned were connected with MDS.

When I arrived at the meeting, Councilman James (not his real name), who was chairing the meetings, immediately approached me, bowed on one knee and apologized for not inviting me to the meetings. His reason was that he simply forgot! I shall never forget the expression on his red face as he made the apology. I was very embarrassed and asked that he get up and that all was forgiven.

Our first application was not accepted so we applied again the following year.

In an effort to jump-start the W & S Program, and confident that it would eventually be funded, on October 12, 2004 Joel Owens, Local Initiative Service Corporation (LISC) Program Officer, convened a meeting with interested W & S members to announce funding of a safety coordinator position.

Mr. Owens stated that because of MDS' prominent position in the Summit neighborhood, the money would be awarded to our agency and I would supervise the Safety Coordinator. It was envisioned that one of the major responsibilities of this position would be to provide staff capacity to the W & S Committee. This person would then be in line to become the W & S Site Coordinator. A job description was developed and the search began. A qualified candidate, Asie Singleton, a retired police officer, was hired to fill the position.

Even though our application was not funded, seven of the Committee members, including Dave and me, continued to meet and plan to apply for the next round of funding. After several attempts, in the summer of 2006, Canton was recognized as a new W & S site.

The Cleveland U.S. Attorney General and several of his staff came to Canton to announce formal recognition of our W & S Program. All of them toured the W & S area and visited the youth and adult safe havens.

The Attorney General was very impressed with our youth safe haven. Even though he was on a very tight schedule, he took time to visit our garden. He said to me, "You have a great safe haven. Now you need some funding and this is where W & S can help!" Wow, this was wonderful news! The MDS programs were mentioned throughout the proposal and, in my opinion, had a positive impact on its being awarded.

After the meeting with the Attorney General and his staff, in an effort to acquire more information and get a better understanding about W & S, Dave Roberts, Asie Singleton and I visited a site in Cleveland, Ohio that had been in existence for several years. We were very impressed with their progress and listened as we were told about their challenges. They were making strides in dealing with the drug and alcohol problems and dilapidated housing. They were also in the process of building new homes.

One thing the Director emphasized is that we should listen to those that reside in the target area. Keep them involved because they are the ones that live with the problems and want things to change. The last thing he said was, "**Do not** let politics drive your program! It has no place in W & S."

We invited the young man to one of our first W & S meetings and he shared this information with those in attendance. After he finished his presentation, our Chairman said, "Well that might be the way you run things in Cleveland, but we're going to do things differently here." And, that is exactly what happened. The Chairman immediately moved from his normal side seat at the conference table to sit at the head of the table and said, "I'm going to run W & S the way we do City Council." The room became so quiet you could hear a pin drop.

His first course of action was to form a Finance Committee. He asked one of the MDS board members to resign from the board so he could use him on the W & S Finance Committee! The W & S chairman was also an MDS board member, but not very active. The Board and I were really surprised at this action particularly when it had not been discussed nor had a formal resignation been sent by the W & S Chairman.

The W & S Committee agreed that a search should be held to elect a W & S Site Coordinator. Asie was the Acting Coordinator. In January, 2007, interviews were held with four final candidates and in February a new site coordinator was elected. It was not Asie. The monthly meetings were lengthy and most of the time disorderly.

There was always a discussion about who were members, why are some names still on the membership list and they have never attended a meeting, etc.

The meetings were so unproductive that our Mayor, Janet Creighton, made it a point to be present so she could restore order and assist the chairperson in running the meeting. We did not have a parliamentarian and the chairman was not familiar with Roberts Rules of Order! As busy as she was, the Mayor took it upon herself to contact every person listed as a W & S Steering Committee member to see if they were still interested in being on the Committee. This was necessary because some of those listed as being committee members had never attended a meeting or had attended only one or two. It was difficult to establish a quorum!

It was the committee's understanding that the W & S program was to be "resident driven." However, there were few residents on the board. I recall one resident in particular that was in attendance at the majority of meetings. However, when she petitioned for membership, the chairman waited until she was absent and then asked for a secret ballot vote. She was voted down.

In the original budget, as the recognized "youth safe haven", MDS requested a van. Our current van, which was donated, had more than 250,000 miles and was unsafe to transport our clients.

The new van would allow us to continue to transport our youth to and from the safe haven, pick up additional youth that were in the W & S area but not close enough to walk to our safe haven, and lastly, deliver food pantry items to the seniors that lived in the area.

It took several months before the funding agency informed us that we could not purchase a van but could lease one. For several meetings, the van was the subject of discussion. The Chairman continued to say he was not in favor of MDS having a van. He wanted to do other things with the money but he never said what he wanted to do nor was he questioned. This issue was never put to a vote, but the Chairman, at every meeting, would say the budget was not ready to be sent to our Cleveland office until we could resolve the van issue. One of the committee members was trying to find another funding source for our van.

I think the most surprising and somewhat painful thing was when the local newspaper indicated that MDS was holding up thousands of dollars from coming into the city because of a "van!" A politically connected friend suggested I call the newspaper for a meeting. I took her advice and requested a meeting with the editor. The meeting was granted. I explained to him exactly what was happening. It was evident that he had already been swayed by someone that MDS was holding up the W & S funds when he looked at me with a stern look on his face and said, "Well, aren't you holding up the funding?" No matter what I said or tried to explain about the actual facts, I was not able to convince him that he did not receive the truth about the van. I thanked him for his time and left.

After this meeting, my board and I decided it was not worth the fight and to let the budget pass without including the van. I said, "God you know we need the van and I know you will provide another source." God always has a back up plan!

Several weeks later, I sent a proposal to a local foundation requesting funds for a van. In the meantime, because the current van MDS owned was not safe, it was necessary for the after-school staff to either walk the children home or transport them in their cars.

Two months after the proposal had been submitted to purchase a van, I received a letter stating that the proposal had been approved.

When I informed the staff that the proposal to purchase a new van had been approved, we began to reflect on previous W & S Meetings involving MDS and the van. We unanimously agreed that there would be less stress because we own the van. We were able to pick up any of our clients and transport them to wherever necessary without someone looking over our shoulders as if we were in violation. I couldn't imagine denying a youth or senior a seat in the van because they were a few blocks out of the W & S area.

One of the great needs in the neighborhood was food. Some of the W & S funding helped support the food pantry that had already been established at MDS. With the additional funding we were able to hire a staff person that allowed us to expand our services and provide not only food but administer a needs assessment. This assessment allowed us to make referrals for job training, drug treatment, medical services and other types of support.

In addition to working with the food pantry, because the staff person had proper credentials, she coordinated our Prostitutes Anonymous Program. MDS had started this program several years ago but because of the drug-related problems decided it was best to transfer the clients to an agency that had trained staff to assist the women. Our new staff person was very instrumental in creating a program for "Johns", men that solicit prostitutes.

I always tell my staff that "when God **BLESSES**, the devil messes." So, without my knowledge, the funding received from W & S that allowed me to hire a staff person to coordinate the food pantry and work on the Prostitutes Anonymous Program, was taken and given to another agency. Ouch! I later learned that several meetings were held with the new agency, the Site Coordinator and W & S Chairperson to discuss taking the program from MDS. Once again, politics raises its ugly head!

Because of the increase in the number of individuals and families that MDS was servicing, without the staff person, there was no one available to manage this program. In 2007, our small agency provided food to 3,078 individuals. Needless to say, we had to close the food pantry. We posted a list of other available food pantries in the county. The majority of clients who were serviced by the food pantry lived within walking distance and did not have transportation to travel to pantries outside the neighborhood. The negative effects of politics always seem to hurt those that are most in need.

It was not enough that we had to close the food pantry, but the W & S Chairman attempted to do additional damage by spreading negative rumors about the agency in an effort to discredit and stop other funding. I was informed, by two reliable sources, that the chairman commented to them that he would make sure MDS did not receive any further funding from the City. Refer back to the chapter on our shelter and how the City cut our funding. My board and I were still trying to understand why the chairman was against MDS.

When we received phone calls or clients walked in to inquire about food, I informed staff to reply that funding was cut and until we could secure another funding source, we would remain closed. I also instructed staff not to give out any information regarding the funding source or why we felt we were cut. I did meet with someone from the newspaper and gave them all of the information regarding the closing of the food pantry, but nothing was written.

I made many attempts to talk with the W & S chairman, but he refused meetings. I even sent him a letter asking for a meeting so we could sit down and try to work through whatever was bothering him about me and the agency—no response! The Mayor and one of her staff met with both of us to see if they could intervene and try to find out what happened to the "wonderful" relationship we once had. The W & S Chairman had nothing to say!

After each incident, my faith increased! I also always remember to pray for those that despitefully use me knowing that God said, "He would make our enemies our footstool!" My Mother always taught me when folks do me wrong to "kill them with kindness" and this I do!

The reimbursement process for W & S was very slow. This added additional problems to our existing budget.

One of our reimbursements was $1,500 short. In speaking with the site coordinator and discussing the shortage, he admitted that an error had been made. He said we should expect to receive the check within two weeks.

Thirty days later we still had not received the check. After 45 days had passed, the MDS bookkeeper called to inquire about the check. The site coordinator apologized and indicated he had been ill but would discuss this with the W & S executive committee.

Thirty more days passed and still no check. We are now in a new fiscal year.

I shall never forget a short time later I saw the site coordinator at a neighborhood meeting. He was very thin and had a sad demeanor as he slowly approached me. He looked me in the eye and said, "Betty I am so sorry that you have not received the $1,500 check that W & S owes MDS. We are now in a new fiscal year and I might have to pay you out of my pocket."

I told him that he should not have to do this because it is not his fault we have not been paid. I continued by reminding him that he has a committee and chairman that must accept part of the responsibility. He just looked at me and again apologized. His final words were, "I've just been in and out of the hospital and not able to handle things the way I should." I told him to take care of himself and not to worry because I was sure something would work out. I felt sorry for him. I saw the W & S chairman at this meeting and felt anger creep into my spirit. It was necessary for me to ask God to forgive me for these feelings.

It is now February 2010 and I am out of touch with W & S, but recently learned that the original Site Coordinator passed away and the W & S Chairperson is now the new Site Coordinator! The $1,500 has still not been paid to MDS. I rest my case!

OTHER MDS PROGRAMS

In addition to the many housing programs, MDS had a variety of programs such as **Black Parenting Classes**. The parenting classes were specifically for mothers attempting to regain custody of their children. Child Protective Services (CPS) referred most of the participants to the class. Some of the topics covered during the classes include parenting techniques, housekeeping, relationships, budgeting, nutrition and meal planning. There was information on alternative housing sources shared also. Participants that did not have custody of their children were given the opportunity, on a weekly basis, to spend time with them during the parenting class.

We also had an Information and Referral Program and a Senior Program called Sip, Soup and Salad that provided an afternoon of networking at our Fulton House. The food was provided by a dear friend who is affectionately called Tommy B, "The Nutty Italian." Rental and Utility assistance was provided by Federal Emergency Management Assistance (FEMA) funds. We also had support from some of our local churches.

For a short time, we had a Boutique that was established to train our youth how to become entrepreneurs. It was short-lived because of funding and not enough volunteers.

One of our loyal supporters was Helen Potillo, a senior citizen who, in spite of being extremely busy with her own business, took time to shop and drop off food items for those in need. Ms Potillo stayed in touch with me at least twice a month. It was nothing unusual for her to call me at 6:30 am. Her kind voice was always so bubbly and cheerful as she would say, "Betty, this is Helen, what do you need." Some of her phone calls were made when she was out of state on business. She would call to inquire about needs for the ladies living in our shelter. Some of the items included beautiful bed linen and sometimes clothing or bath essentials. MDS has other supporters such as Stephanie and Darcy that would often call or drop off donations.

Brandon Talbert—Canton Idol

Rachel Crozier—Canton Idol

The next four programs are referred to as "Signature" events.

CANTON IDOL

In 2002, a resident in the Summit neighborhood met with me to discuss a fundraising project that would support our programs. His idea was to have a "Canton Idol" competition. I informed him that his idea was a good one but, at that time, there were no available staff to assist. He responded by saying that he would put together a committee. The announcement was made about Canton Idol and two weeks later the young man informed me that his job was transferring him out of state. Oh, no!

Because the announcement was made and the Agency's name was connected, I had no choice but to follow through. The response was overwhelming, more than 100 applicants registered for the competition. The Repository was one of our sponsors. Margie Centrone and her staff were very helpful.

Every year thereafter we have been successful in getting parents and friends to volunteer. Jack Wadsworth was our first choreographer. He was once a choreographer for the June Taylor Dancers. This goes way back in time, but those my age and older will surely remember those outstanding dancers.

The last several years, MDS has been **BLESSED** with a group of faithful volunteers. They are the Crozier family (Brad, Christa, Rachel and Dominic) and Vicky Thewes. Tony Barrino has faithfully assisted backstage. Without the help of these wonderful people, it would be impossible to continue Canton Idol.

Canton Idol continues to grow with applicants that are truly gifted and just want an opportunity to perform. The majority of them say, "It is not about the money, I just love to sing." However, some of the performances come with a stipend which contestants graciously accept.

To date, we have auditioned more than 700 singers and have a rotating group that sings at many functions throughout Stark County, Ohio. Some of our performers have formed bands and are touring, some have auditioned for American Idol. One made it to Hollywood! Others have won local competitions.

We also have "future" Canton Idol performers that are as young as four. One of our "future" performers, McKenzie Mac, at age five performed at the Apollo Theatre in New York. We are expecting great things from her in the future.

DOWNTOWN NU-ZONE

MDS' 1002 building has a 2.3 acre lot so I decided to see if there was a possibility of turning it into a neighborhood arts venue. I called a meeting with two friends, Jack Wadsworth and Lois DiGiacomo of Rainbow Repertory, to discuss what kind of programs might work. This area has a lot of drugs and prostitutes and is known as "the Newton Zone." Newton is the name of the street where a lot of this activity takes place.

We decided to change the name to Downtown NU-Zone. There was an outpouring of support from local performing artists and 2nd April Art Galerie owners, Todd Walburn and Brennis Booth, convinced some of their artists to partner by bringing their artwork, jewelry, or whatever they had to display. While this was not a money-making venture, the networking and resident support was phenomenal.

There was also great support from Mayor Richard Watkins and his successor Mayor Janet Creighton. It is always a good thing when the city takes a concerned interest in neighborhoods, which in my opinion are the backbone of any city.

We were very aware that prostitutes were in the neighborhood, but you did not know it because they never showed up when we were having any of our events. Well, let me change that. I had a neighbor whisper in my ear that at several of our events she saw one of the prostitutes with her children participating in the children's activities. The neighbor said, "I've never seen her actively involved with her children in anything positive until now." Thank you God!

Of course we had our skeptics and some that didn't like the neighborhood. Instead of supporting, they would just have negative things to say, but that is expected in anything you do that is positive so we were not discouraged.

For four years the Downtown NU-Zone was held in the Summit neighborhood. The fifth year we partnered with Joe Paris, Founder and Executive Director of KidSummit against Drugs. The Saturday before Father's Day, Joe's agency always planned a program for fathers and their children. He had already made arrangements to have his event in downtown Canton so it was decided to keep that arrangement. The Summit neighborhood is within walking distance of downtown.

The Downtown NU-Zone made a positive impact on the Summit neighborhood.

GOSPEL JOINS SYMPHONY

In 2004, I became a member of the Canton Symphony Orchestra Board and was very excited about the possibility of involving more African-Americans. I attended a fantastic concert in Akron called "Gospel Meets Symphony." It was simply outstanding and brought back to memory the concerts my Chicago church had every year at Christmas and Easter. The thing that impressed me most about "Gospel Meets Symphony" was their minority outreach division. There are very few African-Americans involved in symphony projects, whether it is playing an instrument or being involved on committees.

Growing up in Logansport, Indiana, we had "music appreciation" classes. That is where I became interested in classical music. I had a few viola lessons but settled for piano and clarinet. During my years in high school, I was a member of the orchestra, marching band and a five piece jazz band called "Four Jacks and a Jill." The latter group was an awesome experience that allowed me to travel, meet some wonderful people and, since we were union members, I was paid a whole $10 per gig! For a teenager that was a lot of money in the mid 50's.

Back to "Gospel Joins Symphony." After attending this event, I became very excited and met with the Executive Director of the Canton Symphony Orchestra about a similar program. I indicated that the role of Minority Outreach Coordinator appealed to me and I would be happy to fill the role if she approved. She explained to me that approximately ten years ago an attempt was made to have a similar concert but it was short lived and, therefore, she did not want to try it again.

Gospel Joins Symphony advertisement

I'm not the kind of person that readily accepts "no" when I feel the proposed program or service is one that will benefit others. The Board and I decided that MDS would use this as an opportunity to become involved with the Symphony and the church community. Now this was a serious leap of faith, since in order to make this happen we needed major sponsors, community support and a "dynamic" choir that would attract attention.

I discussed this with a good friend of mine who was a member of the music department at my former church, the Apostolic Church of God. He thought it was a great idea and that I should discuss it with the Pastor, Bishop Brazier.

I drove to Chicago and met with Bishop. We discussed the concert and the impact I felt it would make on the Stark County, Ohio community. I then asked for his support. Bishop said, "I think we can do this but not right away." I commented that the following year would be fine. Bishop gave me the okay sign and said he would meet with his Minister of Music.

After Bishop met with his Minister of Music, Mark Jordan, I planned another trip to Chicago. Mark was excited and said that when Bishop spoke to him his words were, "Mark, make this happen." When Mark discussed it with the choir he had more than 300 responses. Yikes! Our stage would only accommodate 200. However, Bruce Ballough, Stage Manager for Umstattd Hall, where the concert would be performed, said he could possibly squeeze in 220.

My next step was to meet with the Executive Director of the Canton Symphony Orchestra to negotiate a contract. Bishop agreed to handle all of the expenses for the choir which included lodging for two nights, transportation and food. However, it was still a challenge to pay for the Symphony but I was not concerned and knew that God would provide. Several proposals were mailed followed up with phone calls and meetings. We had positive responses from the Timken Foundation, several churches and others.

It was now time for the MDS board and a six-member committee to put the implementation plan into action. Su Nimon, a local artist now housed at 2nd April Art Galerie, 324 Cleveland Ave., was excited about designing the logo and all marketing materials. Justine Chenault, a Canton City Schools music teacher, singer and flutist, agreed to form a flute choir that would entertain in the lobby before the concert started. I gently twisted Terrance

Jones arm and he agreed to supply 15 hosts and hostesses. Mr. Nate Pope agreed to be our chairperson.

District Elder Ralph Byrd, Pastor of Greater Bethel Apostolic Church, agreed to pay for the reception and offered the services of Mary Smith, one of his staff. Mary assisted with the program book, marketing and other administrative duties.

There was a lot of excitement, phone calls, contracts, scheduling, meetings, etc. to make this night happen. In the meantime, the current Executive Director of the Symphony retired and a new one was hired. It was a smooth transition.

Out of the clear blue, I received a phone call from Johnny Davis, the first Director of our L.I.F.E. Program. After playing catch up on what was happening at MDS and in his life, I told him about Gospel Joins Symphony. Johnny became excited and said, "Betty, you must get in touch with a young lady named Dana Morgan from Warren Ohio, not far from Canton. She is an outstanding pianist and would be perfect for this concert."

Johnny gave me the information. I made a phone call and spoke with Dana's mother, Gwen. Dana was away in college at Howard University. After talking with Gwen for a few minutes, I learned that she was once a member of the famous gospel groups, "The Caravans". I told her one of the original and still performing singers in this group is a very good friend of mine, Albertina Walker. Gwen and I talked for an hour.

Gwen indicated she would contact Dana to see if it would be possible for her to participate on the program. Several days later Gwen called with a very strong affirmative answer for Dana to appear.

On September 23, 2005, Chicago took Canton by storm with 220 choir members, 20 musicians, 25 other supporters, Bishop Brazier and a very dear friend of mine, Mrs. Delores Jordan.

The choir had a few hours to refresh themselves and then loaded their buses to attend the rehearsal. The rehearsal was so astounding that it drew the attention of many of the students that were in the lunchroom at McKinley High School. The Symphony's concerts are held in the school's auditorium known as Umstattd Hall. I listened to the comments as the students came rushing into the auditorium. "Wow, what choir is singing?" "What orchestra is playing?" "When will they be singing?" "I wonder if I can get a ticket." I was so excited that I gave all those that were in the rehearsal hall and wanted to attend the concert a complimentary ticket, approximately 30.

There are no words to describe the performance by Dana Morgan, the Apostolic Church of God Choir and the Canton Symphony Orchestra. The youth said, "It was off the hook, off the chain." One of my Jewish friends said, "Betty, I never liked Gospel music until tonight. One of the male soloists should be traveling around the country singing. He sounds like an opera singer." Several told me they cried throughout the performance. Every song received a "standing ovation." Many still ask, "When are you bringing back that awesome choir from Chicago"?

After the concert, phone calls, emails and cards poured into the office. I will share a few of them with you:

What a fabulous evening showcasing the diversity of our community. Much more than I ever dreamed, and there is a loud chorus of encore for next year!! Job well done and appreciated.

Mayor Janet Creighton

Canton has always been known for Friday night football. We have the Football Hall of Fame to prove that, but the Gospel Joins Symphony has brought class and culture to our City. Uplifting for our young people to see and hear this outstanding event. What else could I say? Just outstanding.

Robert Fisher, CPA, Fisher & Fisher Associates

Mrs. Smith, I wanted to congratulate you and your organization on an excellent performance Friday evening. I want to personally congratulate and give you credit for being courageous enough to take that big step to introduce this event to the Canton community. We had a lovely evening. Good luck in the future and God Bless.

Brenda L. Justice, Akron Symphony Orchestra Staff

I was truly blessed to come home and enjoy such a heartfelt program here in Canton, Ohio,—the Gospel Joins Symphony. As I tried to stay on the edge of my seat, tears flowed and joy filled my heart. Mrs. Betty Smith, such a giving and delightful God anointed person. Let His presence be with you and to continue to bless your Agency. Until next year, I will be back and will bring some friends.

Brenda K. Washington (Kennesaw, GA)

This was a very well organized, professional concert. One which the orchestra member enjoyed being a part of. We were not sure what to expect of the choir or its Director, but when we met Mr. Mark Jordan and heard the choir at rehearsal, we knew they were professional in all aspects.

Marie-Hélène Bernard, Executive Director, Canton Symphony Orchestra

Betty, the concert was outstanding. All of those in my party thoroughly enjoyed it. Do it again!

Chip Conde, Bicentennial Coordinator

It was an outstanding event and one I shall never forget.

Pastor Robert Dye, AME Church

Thank you so much for bringing such an awesome event "Gospel Joins Symphony" to the Canton community. It was a most awesome presentation. To God is the glory. He gave you the faith, the patience, and the strength to bring such a wonderful blessing to us. Ain't no stopping you now! Smile.

Gwendolyn Singleterry, Retired—Member of SWAN Community Organization

Very spiritual and uplifting. The combination of the sound of voices from the Chicago Apostolic Church of God Choir and the instruments from the Canton Symphony Orchestra was awesome . . . . A very memorable experience enjoyed by a diverse group of people. Looking forward to the next concert.

Ann Lancaster

Betty, you are so creative and good for our community. Thank you very much for bringing this event to Canton. It was most enjoyable.

Ellen Beidler, Executive Director, Herbert W. Hoover Foundation

This was a first class event and I was very impressed and had a wonderful time. I bought tickets and gave them to some of my friends. All of them had nothing but words of excitement and enthusiasm as they talked about the evening.

Mrs. Hortense Bobbitt, Owner, McDonald's Restaurants

Doing good is its own reward. Thank you for bringing Gospel Joins Symphony to Canton. It was wonderful, a sentiment also shared by the friends I invited.
Barbara Currence, Minority Outreach for Cancer Society

Betty, this was simply outstanding. Because of football traffic, we were somewhat late and decided we would leave early to beat the crowd. When we heard the first song and the outstanding soloist, my guests and I looked at one another and said almost simultaneously "we are not leaving early."
Nancy Knudsen, Executive Director, Timken Foundation

The following year we formed a community choir and "Chip" Johnson, agreed to fly in, rehearse the choir, and conduct the choir and symphony. Now this was quite a task, but Chip was a man of his word and did just that. This particular year we had the support of the Malone College choir (50) voices that proved to be our anchor choir. We were not able to attract a lot of singers from the area, but with the help of Malone we had a full choir in place.

I also contracted with three singers from the Apostolic Church of God Choir and several musicians from outside Canton to accompany the choir. One of the challenges was finding musicians that could not only read music but could also play Gospel.

Our second Gospel Joins Symphony was a great concert. Lisa Walters, the young lady I wrote about in an earlier chapter, is an accomplished musician and was our special guest. She not only plays the piano, but sings and writes music. Her major in college was Ethnomusicology. *Ethnomusicology* is a branch of musicology defined as "the study of social and cultural aspects of music and dance in local and global contexts."

The third and fourth Gospel Join Symphony concerts featured the Wilberforce University Choir conducted by Jeremy Winston. They were outstanding and blessed us with their repertoire of gospel, hymns and classical music.

Because we were unable to get necessary funding or enough of the churches to provide support, it was in our best interest to discontinue Gospel Joins Symphony until a later date.

My years as a Symphony board member have enriched my life. I have served with men and women from various backgrounds that have given dedicated service to one of the finest orchestras in the country.

Maestro Gerhardt Zimmerman is a one of a kind conductor. In 2011, he will celebrate his 30th year Anniversary with the Canton Symphony Orchestra. For additional information, log on to www.cantonsymphony. org.

GOLDEN DOVE AWARDS

During the first year of operation we acquired five pieces of property, received funding from numerous foundations and had a host of friends and supporters. I always believe in giving people flowers while they can smell them, so I proposed to the Board, and they agreed, that it would be appropriate to have an awards celebration. We gave some of them a "Golden Dove Award" and others plaques. Those that received the "Golden Dove Award" would be "unsung heroes." These are persons that went above and beyond the call of duty in their line of work. We also presented plaques to individuals, foundations and others that provided financial support to MDS.

For five years, Herald "Chip" Johnson from Chicago was the guest emcee. He was simply wonderful and had such a great sense of humor. I remember the first year he was not the emcee many of our regular supporters said, "What happened to Chip!" So you see Chip, Canton loves you.

During my second year of producing the Golden Dove Awards, I was very surprised and grateful to receive an editorial congratulating me for honoring such wonderful citizens of Stark County.

Mrs. Deloris Jordan was our special guest for our Third Annual Golden Dove Awards.

The next three years our Golden Dove Awards emcee was Attorney John Werren. In addition to being an outstanding attorney, he is quite a historian and has a wonderful sense of humor. I first met John when I was a member of the Community Services of Stark County Board. He, too, was a member.

Chip Johnson and Betty—Golden Dove Awards

In 2009, the Golden Dove Awards celebrated ten years of honoring more than 100 outstanding individuals, including Mayors, agency directors, agency supervisors, line staff, community builders, women making a difference and others.

Dominion East Ohio and the Repository were faithful supporters of this event.

In 2006, I was accepted into the Leadership Stark County Program. The mission is to develop a core of motivated leaders with a lifelong commitment to community trusteeship through training in leadership skills and education about the community. This was an excellent opportunity for me to learn more about Stark County and meet some wonderful people.

The local media was very good at using our press releases or giving us public service announcements.

MDS media friends from the Repository are Charita, Denise, Dan, Diane and Ed. We also receive great support from Gary at MY101.7, Fred from WHBC 1390 and Bobbi at the Oasis Network, 88.7.

GOD WAS TRYING TO TELL ME SOMETHING, BUT I DIDN'T LISTEN

In 2007, I felt God showing me signs of my second retirement and I was really ready to step down as Executive Director. However, I always had one more project that needed to be completed before this could happen. I continued working 80 hours a week all the while telling myself it was time to step down. I was really feeling the wear and tear on my body, but I kept working. I'm sure many of you reading this can relate. God was really trying to give me a message, but I did not heed the warning.

One thing about God, when He can't get your attention one way, He will get it another. I know there is probably a lot of controversy on this subject, but I'm going on what I believe. This is my story about how God got my attention.

During the summer of 2008, two of my girlfriends, Claudette Hankins and Becky Helaney, and her husband Joe and I began training to walk a half-marathon in Columbus, Ohio.

Claudette and I walked this Marathon in 2007 as well as the Cleveland Marathon in May.

In September, for our half-marathon training, we walked 11 miles. After returning home from the walk, I became very dizzy. This was on a Sunday morning and my husband had already left for church. I felt myself getting ready to faint, so I dropped to the floor, crawled to the telephone and dialed the number at the church. My husband had not made it to the church so I left word for him to come home as soon as he walked in the door.

When he arrived home, I was lying on the floor still conscious and asked him to help me to the sofa. I was very thirsty and drank two gallons of water. You might say I was dehydrated. There was also a great deal of pain in my right arm.

On September 8th, I had an appointment with my chiropractor, Dr. Scott Snow. Dr. Snow has been my chiropractor since I moved to Canton in 1998. He attended one of the same schools as my Chicago Chiropractor, Dr. Dennis Prowell. Therefore, I felt very comfortable with his treatments. Whenever I was in Chicago, approximately every 3 or 4 months, I would schedule an appointment with Dr. Prowell. There were times when he had to "squeeze" me in because I had not given him sufficient notice. He never failed to see me. In addition to being a chiropractor, Dr. Prowell is also a Napropath. Napropathy is a drugless method of treatment based on the belief that disease symptoms arise from problems with ligaments and connective tissue. He often would tell me that he needed to use both forms of treatment on me. I guess my body is really complex. LOL (laugh out loud).

Dr. Snow's treatments for my arm pain only provided temporary relief. Because the relief was only temporary, he recommended that I have an x-ray. He also suggested massotherapy. A dear friend of mine, Joan Gillespie, recommended Barb Bellassai, who turned out to be a **Blessing in the midst of my pain**! Joan is the kind of friend that always has an ear to hear, hands to help, a compassionate heart and one that tells you just like it is. There is no guessing with Joan. To me, that's the meaning of a true friend.

As recommended by Dr. Snow, I had an x-ray. The results showed I had a herniated disk, C7, (cervical vertebra). C7 is the symbol for the 7th cervical (neck) vertebral bone (C7) which is sometimes called the prominent vertebra due to the length of its spinous process (the projection off the back of the vertebral body.) This herniated disk was causing my pain. I was determined to walk the marathon so I began to do a lot of stretching exercises and applying hot and cold packs on my back and arm and prayed for strength. I began to feel better and stepped out on faith to walk this marathon.

In October, we walked the marathon and I finished in 3 hours and 2 minutes. The previous year I finished in 2 hours and 54 minutes and was first in my age category. I did not experience any pain during the race. Within two weeks after the race, I began to experience severe pain in my right arm. My two middle fingers were numb which made it difficult to navigate the mouse on my computer. Sometimes I would try to force my fingers to function so I could respond to emails. I was determined to work in spite of my body telling me to slow down. This reminded me of something my mother used to say, "A hard head makes a soft behind"!

In spite of my pain, I was determined to work. I continued my chiropractic treatments with Dr. Snow. On November 10th, I had a severe headache and my husband took me to the ER. The ER doctor gave me a prescription for pain and told me to make an appointment with my primary care physician.

On November 11th and 17th, I met with my primary care physician who ordered a series of tests hoping that one of them would explain my headaches. On November 19th, and before my tests, I, once again, was taken to the ER. They gave me an EEG and a CT, but everything was normal. While this was definitely a **BLESSING**, the mystery was still finding the cause for my headaches.

My MRI was scheduled for November 26^{th,} the day before Thanksgiving. Every Thanksgiving, my husband and I travel to Indiana to dine and enjoy the company of my mother and other family members. I was in pain the entire time but was able to "fake" it through the day. I did not want to ruin the day for my family.

My Brother, Fred, was seriously ill and had recently checked into a local nursing home. I was afraid he would not be able to dine with us but his very loving and dedicated son Jeff, flew in from Orange County, California to be with the family, went to the nursing home and picked up his dad.

Fred seemed to enjoy himself even though he was very frail and coughed a lot. I will never forget before I got ready to leave, I was on my way into the kitchen, the favorite spot for the family to sit, laugh and just enjoy one another; Fred gently grabbed my hand, looked at me with his weak eyes and said "I love you".

I said, "I love you too". I then felt sadness as if this was the last time I would see him alive. Fred passed away in February, 2010.

The trip home was very painful. Upon arriving in Canton, my husband drove me to the ER. Since I had just had an MRI, the doctor had access to the results. They were normal! The doctor gave me some pain pills and told me to follow up with my primary care physician.

On December 15th, my primary care physician referred me to a physical therapy team. After the fifth session, I left feeling worse than when I went in so I decided not to return. I spoke with my niece, Celena from Connecticut, who is also a PT. She explained that there was a possibility I was left in traction a little too long which caused my pain. I also spoke by phone with Dr. Prowell who concurred with Celena.

In the meantime, my primary care physician was attempting to schedule an appointment with a neurologist. The first available appointment was not until mid-January, 2009. Because of the intensity of my pain, I prayed and wrote the doctor a letter explaining my condition. There was a lot of snow on the ground, the wind was blowing, and it was a day everyone should have been home. I braved the weather and hand carried the letter to the doctor's office. Within an hour, I received a phone call from the doctor's office with an appointment for December 23rd. What an **UNEXPECTED BLESSING in the Midst of My Pain**! While we're trying to figure it out, God has already worked it out.

When I explained my symptoms to the neurologist, he said to me, "Oh this doesn't sound like anything major. I'm going to prescribe some medication and then refer you to our Neurocare Center." It's interesting how some doctors tell us our pain is minor when we are a minute away from screaming and feel like punching him/her out! Sometimes I think they see so many patients they become immune to anyone complaining about pain!

At 6:00 a.m. on Christmas, I awoke with severe pain in my right arm. This was worse than any previous pain. I lasted as long as I could and finally asked my husband to take me to the ER. They gave me a shot of morphine and said, "This should at least get you through the day and on the next business day, contact your primary care physician." We were scheduled to have Christmas dinner with our friends, the Hankins. I was so grateful to be out of pain so I could enjoy Claudette's wonderful cooking and Robb's great sense of humor.

The ER doctor was right; the shot did get me through the day. At 9:00 p.m., I began to feel very dizzy and sat on the side of the bed. I told my husband I felt as if I was going to faint. The next thing I remember was opening my eyes and looking up at my husband who was bent over me. He said, "You just slid off the bed and I prayed waiting for you to open your eyes." Thank God for a praying husband!

On December 31st, I had the following tests: muscle, two limbs; two motor nerve conductions; six sense nerve conductions; and, two motor nerve conductions. These tests did not show any type of nerve damage that would cause me to have the type of headache pain that I was experiencing. In the meantime, I was still having headaches. My primary care physician continued to send me to various specialists who were trying to determine the cause of my pain.

The first of January, I had an appointment with my massotherapist. On this particular day, I was in so much pain it was difficult to get on the massage table. Barb was so caring and concerned. She took great care of me and her treatment gave me some temporary relief. She then said, "Betty, I hate to see you suffering so I'm going to attempt to contact a physical therapist that used to practice in Akron. I will call you if and when

I can reach him." It always makes me feel very blessed when someone takes more time than normal and goes that extra mile.

Within two days, Barb called and said she had located the PT. She gave me his number and on January 29, 2009, I had my first appointment with Mark Crank who was now working in Canton for Spectrum Orthopedics located at Aultman Hospital. Mark was not only a PT, but he was a genuine, concerned and caring person. When I first saw him, he had such a nonchalant look on his face I had my doubts about his ability. Just proves the old saying, "You can't judge a book by looking at its cover."

Mark and I spent a lot of time together, three sessions a week for six weeks. I was able to share some things about me and my life. During one of the sessions, he was demonstrating some of the exercises that would strengthen my right arm and muscles. I said to him, "Mark, these are some of the exercises I used to teach when conducting my stretching classes." In 1981 I had an exercise studio in Chicago called "Stretchnastics." Mark's reply was, "Well, Betty you know what your problem is?" I just gave him a blank stare and he said, "You should have continued doing the exercises and you most likely would not be in my office. I think you are the kind of person that takes care of others first. Now I think you need to start taking care of yourself, don't you?"

Well, what could I say? He was exactly right and I said to myself that I know that is what God has been saying to me, "Take care of yourself!" Slow down. Quit working 80 hours a week, fool." Now, I added "fool." I don't think God said that, but He has a great sense of humor so He might have used the word "fool."

In social work, and I'm sure other professions, we sometimes get so caught up in taking care of the needs of others that we often neglect ourselves. This is a terrible mistake but one I can talk about now that I am finally in the driver's seat of where I need to be in life.

After I had been in PT with Mark for three weeks, I began to have severe headaches, which in my mind was associated with the herniated disk. I began to complain to Mark, who gave me temporary relief with some of his PT techniques and using some of the same stretching exercises that I used to teach.

During one of my sessions, Mark said, "Betty, I'm not a doctor but I don't think your headaches have anything to do with your herniated disk. I think the headaches are coming from C1-2-3 vertebrae." None of the doctors, to date, had given this diagnosis so I could not comment on Mark's speculation.

Whenever I would say to Mark that I was sick, he would say, "Betty, you have not been diagnosed with a disease so don't say you are sick, just say you are hurting." I always remember that when my head begins to ache.

In the meantime, I'm going from doctor to doctor to get relief from the headaches as Mark continues to treat my right arm, which was getting better and better.

My primary care physician was still desperately trying to get me to the right doctor to find the cause of my headaches. She was very concerned and I could tell she was a bit upset at being unable to help me find the cause for my discomfort. By now I had been prescribed propoxphene, topomax, ibupropen, cyclobenzaprine, alprazolam, prednisone, tramadol, darvocet, lyrica, which made me feel as if I was crazy, lidocaine patch, that did not work, and celebrex, that I took for a short period of time. I have never been much of a pill taker so I was becoming very upset by all of the various medications that were being prescribed. Even though these medications were prescribed, because my body had such a negative reaction to the four pills, I decided not to try the others.

After nothing was working to relieve my pain, I reached out to some of my friends that are acquainted with holistic remedies. This has always been my choice. However, I am not discounting medications that are necessary for some illnesses and diseases. Thank God for doctors that really care and go that extra mile to help their patients. I appreciate you and I don't envy your job.

My friend Joanne Fritsche, a nurse at Aultman, one of our local hospitals, shared with me her struggle with Fibromyalgia. She introduced me to the pressure pump and showed me some of the exercises she would do every evening before going to bed. Joanne periodically checks on me and assures me that things will get better.

The end of January I was referred to another specialist regarding my headaches that was still thought to be associated with my herniated disk. After reviewing my records and talking to me about my condition, he referred me to a doctor that I will call "Doctor A" for an epidural.

On February 17th, I met with the specialist who was to give me an epidural. When I explained my symptoms and talked about the terrible headaches, he immediately informed me that he would not give me the epidural because it would only make my headache worse. He then wanted to know if I had told the referring doctor about my headaches. I replied that I had. Doctor A just shook his head and once again repeated that he would not give me an epidural. I also mentioned to Doctor A that I called the referring doctor's office to let him know that my shoulder and arm was much better but the headaches had intensified. The doctor informed me that I should still have the epidural!

Doctor A strongly suggested that I immediately call the Cleveland Clinic. I thanked him and shook his hand. This doctor could have given me the epidural since he had an order to do such, which probably would have left me in more pain than I was initially experiencing. I thank God for doctors such as this one that was honest enough to let me know he was not the kind of doctor I needed and then referred me to another doctor.

I immediately telephoned the Cleveland Clinic and as only God would have it, I was given an appointment the following day!

On February 18th, I was seen by "Doctor B" at the Cleveland Clinic. He had not received my x-rays but listened intently as I described my pain and the various doctors I had seen. Doctor B had a great sense of humor and put me at ease as he, in a very short period of time, said, "Well, I think I know what you have, but am a bit hesitant. Doctor B looked at me with a puzzled look on his face and said, "The diagnosis I'm going to give you is one not associated with African-Americans!" Well this was a shocker to me. He continued by saying, "But it is also very clear to me that based on your symptoms and the kind of pain you are describing, you have *occipital neuralgia!*" Of course I had never heard of this and did not have a clue as to what it was.

OCCIPITAL NEURALGIA

Occasionally, either the C2 or C3 nerve root can get pinched as it leaves the spine. These are mostly sensory nerve roots, and if they are pinched it can cause a chronic headache. Pain is generally felt in the back of the head or the occipital region.

One cause of chronic headaches that is often overlooked is occipital neuralgia. Occipital Neuralgia is a type of headache that generally begins in the neck and then spreads up through the back of the head, causing throbbing, piercing pain. Often the scalp becomes tender, and sufferers may experience pain behind the eyes and become sensitive to light. Many people describe the pain as migraine-like, and the acute *symptoms* of Occipital Neuralgia can be at least as severe as those caused by a migraine.

Occipital Neuralgia can be caused by injury or irritation to the occipital nerves, which travel up from where the spine connects with the neck to the back of the head. Trauma to the back of the head or nerves compressed by swollen or tight neck muscles are the most common causes of this type of headache. Pressure on the occipital nerves can result in a worsening of symptoms, and physical tension often triggers an attack.

I asked Doctor B what he thought caused me to have Occipital Neuralgia. After asking me a lot of questions, he concluded it was probably from excessive use of the computer. Occipital Neuralgia can also be caused by a downward motion with your head and a forward motion with your shoulders. I could definitely relate to this posture. Every night I would spend four to six hours, non-stop, at the computer. If this sounds like something you do, my advice is to discontinue this at once. It is not worth the pain that it could later cause.

Doctor B explained that he was going to give me a nerve block behind my left and right ear. He placed his finger on the bony part behind my left ear to show me exactly where he was going to put the needle. This was definitely the spot for the worse part of my pain. (I want to interject that I can recall having pain behind my right ear off and on for about 20 years. I would treat it with hot and cold packs and chiropractic care. It never lasted longer than a day.) After the injection, he said it would immediately numb the lower part of my head and relieve the pain. I was then instructed to return in three months for another nerve block. He said he did not believe in giving too many and would probably only give me three. I asked Doctor B if I should continue visits with my chiropractor and he said "No!"

After Doctor B gave me the diagnosis of Occipital Neuralgia, my mind went back to what Mark Crank had said, "Betty, I don't think your headaches have anything to do with your herniated disk; I think they are caused by C1-2-3 vertebrae!" Mark, you were right!

I was feeling very jubilant that finally someone had given me a diagnosis and I was going to get better. I thought! My husband and I left the office and visited one of my favorite restaurants to celebrate. After we finished our meal, I told my husband that I was not numb as Doctor B explained. Later that evening my headache returned. The following day I called the office of Doctor B. It took approximately 1½ weeks for someone to return my call. I explained that the nerve block did not work. The voice on the other end was apologetic and told me she would relay the information to the doctor. Another week went by before Doctor B called. I explained how the nerve block did not work and my headaches were not better. He said he wanted me to get an appointment at the Clinic to have a "Radio Frequency Ablation (RFA)".

I said, "A what!" He explained that it was an implant that would be placed in my neck to help stop the headaches. I thanked him knowing that this procedure was not for me. So I did not schedule the appointment.

After the diagnosis, I said, "God, I know there is a reason for everything that happens so I'm going to take these headaches as a sign that you want me to change direction in my life." The two biggest changes were I knew it was time for me to retire and the other is I am to use this diagnosis of "occipital neuralgia" as a teaching tool to help others. And, as my husband always says when he prays for me, "God, you get the glory out of what my wife is going through."

I then said, "God, I got the message now can you please stop the headaches?" Well, the headaches continued.

My headaches were so severe that I was unable to ride in a car for more than 30 minutes. My husband and I had scheduled a March trip to Las Vegas to support my niece Dr. Joni Flowers' Cultural Diversity Foundation's Annual Scholarship Benefit, but we had to cancel. Joni was very understanding but I was so disappointed knowing how hard she had worked on this event and looked forward to seeing Mark and me. We are very proud of Joni. Check out her website at *www.cdfnv.org*. (Joni is my brother Fred's daughter.)

One thing I know about God is if He gives you a message, it is in your best interest to listen and then follow His direction. Now I haven't always done this and suffered the consequences. I would not recommend suffering God's consequences to anyone, so be obedient when He gives you a directive. The Bible says, "Obey is better than sacrifice."

After receiving the diagnosis and fully understanding what was happening, I knew the first thing I had to do was heed God's warning received in 2007, so I contacted my Agency's Board of Directors and informed them it was time for me to retire. Of course they were in shock and frankly didn't believe me. It took some convincing and a lot of meetings for them to understand that I was serious. So a plan of action was put into place to find my successor. This plan of action is described in another chapter.

Since I refused the RFA recommended by Doctor B, I returned to my primary care physician who was by now pretty perplexed and not sure what the next step should be.

The headaches continued and I was not getting anything but prescriptions for my pain. I said, "God, I do not want to take this medication so I am relying on you to either cure me or help me endure the pain."

I suppose some of you who might be doubters are saying, "If your faith is so great, why didn't God just heal you." Instant healing is not always in His plan. Sometimes there are other things God wants to accomplish through our pain. I have been in many situations when God did heal me, if not instantly, then within a very short period of time.

Let me digress a little and share with you some instances when God did heal me. I have only told a few people about what I call "miracles". I vividly remember when I had severe stomach pain for several months. One morning I woke up and heard the word "cancer"! I had not been feeling well for several months and decided not to go to a doctor, but just pray. I prayed and said, "God heal me, please heal me." I got myself together, went to work and kept praying for God to heal me so I could continue to do His work. I kept repeating, "By your stripes I am healed." I remember going to the bathroom and passing a very large clot of blood that appeared to have strings on it. I heard God say, "You are healed." I'm sure if I had told some folks this, they would not have believed me, so when I find it necessary to minister to certain individuals, I share this story. I received my healing right in the ladies' room. I had no more pain.

Let me share another miracle with you. When I was in my late 20's, I was hospitalized for severe stomach pain. The doctor ordered many tests and upon receiving the results told me I had numerous things wrong with my stomach. He was very concerned. Several years earlier I had an ulcer but after proper treatment, the ulcer was healed. The doctor told me that the recent x-rays showed an ulcer.

After a week and much prayer, I began to feel better but the doctor told me he could not release me because of the findings on the x-rays. At the beginning of the second week, I remember Bishop; at that time he was Elder, Brazier coming to visit me. I told him about the x-rays, but I was really feeling great. He said, "Betty, do you think you've been healed?" I said, "Yes sir, I do." He said, "Then tell the doctor you would like to be discharged."

I spoke to the doctor and informed him that I wanted to be discharged because I was no longer ill. He once again stated that he could not discharge me because of the findings on the x-ray. I kept insisting that I was no longer ill. I didn't tell him that God healed me because I thought this would only delay my discharge. However, he did re-run all of the tests. He was in TOTAL shock when the x-rays showed none of the original problems. He said he did not even see a scar from the ulcer. When I asked if I could be discharged, he said, "I must keep you longer so I can try to figure out what is going on."

I decided it was time to tell him that "God healed me." Of course he did not want to hear this, but several days later I was discharged.

Now back to my Occipital Neuralgia story.

On March 21st, I began to have heart palpitations and went to the ER. Because of my age, they did not want to take any chances so they kept me overnight. During this time, I had a series of tests that included a stress test. Everything came out negative, so I was released the next day.

In addition to the headaches, I began to experience sleepless nights. Sometimes I would go three and four nights without sleep. I spoke to several people that had migraines and fibromyalgia. Of course everyone has different remedies and you must pick and choose those that you think might work.

I took the advice from my friend Joanne, and went to see "Doctor C". He is often out of the office due to his travels and lectures but was able to see me on April 10th. After listening to my story and reviewing my x-rays, he felt I had "upper cervical facet arthritis". He referred me for more x-rays and also to "Doctor D" for an injection that could possibly stop the pain. Before visiting Doctor D on April 11th, I had an x-ray of my neck and spine.

On April 27th, I visited Doctor D and described my symptoms of the pain/pressure in my head, etc. After listening to me and having received a copy of the April 11th x-ray, he told me the injection he was going to give was not what I needed.

Doctor D thought perhaps my headaches might be caused by being on hormones for a long period of time, 28 years on Premarin. He referred me to "Doctor E" who handles women's hormone health issues. Doctor E also suggested I try acupuncture.

In the meantime, I'm still having problems sleeping. One night I tried lying on my back, and a pain originated from the lower part of the left side of my spine all the way to the top of my head. This intense pain lasted for approximately 30 minutes. The top of my head was very sore. It took another three hours for the soreness in my head to diminish.

Many nights when I was unable to sleep, I would sit in the living room and pray and sometimes cry. My good friend, Dr. HelenVallier, would often call me around 5:00 or 5:30 a.m., 4:00 and 4:30 a.m. Chicago time, knowing I would be awake. She would be preparing for work. There were also times I would call her for prayer and comfort. This helped get me through many critical days when I knew I would be like a zombie because of lack of sleep.

Several other long-time friends of mine from Chicago, Calvita Fredrick-Sowell, Dawn Joi who refers to me as "Betty Mac from way back", Vel, Sasha, Kitty and Kay Robinson, always sent me words of comfort via email. Kay would often call and just pray with me.

On May 5th, I met with Doctor E who ordered a battery of blood tests that would give him an indication about my hormonal condition. I went for the tests. They took three large vials of blood from me. I had never had this much blood drawn in my life. This test yielded five pages of results.

Following up on the other recommendation from Doctor D, I made an appointment to see an acupuncturist, "Doctor F." My visit was on May 7th. I explained to Doctor F the difficulty with my headaches and inability to sleep. He stuck me with a lot of needles, which did not have any kind of effect on my headaches or ability to sleep. He told me I would need a minimum of five appointments before I would feel any relief. I went for the second treatment and was very annoyed that I was left with the needles in me for an extended period of time before he came to check on me. I was unable to signal him because I was lying on my stomach. The door was closed so he could not hear me when I kept shouting his name. So, the third visit I took my husband with me. After "Doctor F" removed the needles, I was extremely weak and could barely walk. However, he did not appear concerned!

Several hours after the treatment, I became extremely sick at my stomach and my head was pounding. I called Doctor F and he said, "Your body is very sick. You need to go see your doctor!" Wow! This was a surprise. Needless to say, I did not return to Doctor F.

The first of June I returned to see Doctor E who told me my hormones were out of balance. He also told me my cholesterol was extremely high. This was not surprising since it has always been high most of my life. High cholesterol runs in my family and most of them are on some type of medication. At one time, I took Lipitor but after being on it for one year I began to have heart palpitations and decided not to take anything else. My HDL is 106 and my LDL is 236. I have always exercised and try to watch my diet. However, with the headaches, during this time I was not able to exercise.

Even though I was in and out of the ER and seeing doctors almost on a weekly basis, I was still working part-time at the Agency I founded until my successor could be identified. In addition, I was the Chairman of the Pro Football Hall of Fame Enshrinement Festival's Fashion Show. This was truly an honor since I was the second African-American to have this volunteer position in the 63-year history of this event. This Fashion Show averages an attendance of 3,700. It was important to me, if at all possible, to fulfill all of my 2009 volunteer commitments.

During my first year as Chairman, I was able to implement two new ideas to the Fashion Show that were readily accepted by the committee and staff. The first new program was a Top Model Competition that was open to non-professionals throughout Northeast Ohio. Winners in each age category would be able to model in the Pro Football Hall of Fame Enshrinement Festival Fashion Show. This was successful so we repeated the competition during my second year as Chairman.

My second new addition to the Festival was the "Fan Fashion Favorite." Several volunteers in each room selected one lady they felt had on an exceptional outfit. These ladies were invited to the main stage and the audience, by means of applause, selected the winner.

It was really ironic that the first time we implemented the Fan Fashion Favorite, my sister-in-law, Frances Bendter, without my knowledge, was selected as one of the six to appear on stage. When I learned of this I was in shock and was hoping that no one knew she was my sister-in-law because they would have thought it was arranged. Luckily this was not the case. Frances was the runner-up in the competition!

I would not have been able to accept this volunteer position if it had not been for the dedicated staff that work for the Stark County Regional Chamber of Commerce. This staff provides much-needed support for all chairpersons. If you have not attended any of these wonderful events, you might want to add this to your vacation schedule. For further information log on to www.cantonchamber.org.

For the past ten years, I have hosted a Canton City Schools TV Show, Channel 11, "On Track with Betty Mac." The wonderful staff made things easier. I give a shout out to Bill, Trent, Jacki and Scott. I continued to do this in spite of my pain. My prayer would always be that I would get enough sleep to be able to interview my guests. There were several times when I had no sleep and had to rely on strong coffee to keep me alert. What a horrible feeling!

Another honor for me was to be selected to serve as a judge for the Pro Football Hall of Fame Enshrinement Festival's Queen's Pageant. The past two years, I served as co-emcee with Kayleigh Kriss from Mix 94.1.

I recall not having any sleep the night before the Pageant. I was so sleepy that I was actually sick to my stomach, but I did not let any of the other judges know just how tired and sick I was. It was by the Grace of God that I was able to make it through the event.

The night before the Fashion Show, I had two hours of sleep and was feeling quite sick. I was concerned about whether or not I would be able to take center stage and welcome the 3,000 plus guests. Rev. Carlos Morris, Pastor of Greater Bethel Apostolic Church, was guest minister for the room I was hosting. Because of the large number of attendees at the Fashion Show, we had six rooms to accommodate our guests. Each room had a host and a guest minister. I told Rev. Morris I had only two hours of sleep the night before and asked that he please keep me in prayer. He said, "Sister Betty, I'm going to pray for you right now." I bowed my head and Rev. Morris prayed. God answered immediately. When it was time for me to take center stage and greet the guests, I briskly moved to the tune "I've Got a New Attitude."

After the Fashion Show, I went home and was able to sleep for 45 minutes. I then showered, changed clothes and my husband and I traveled 15 minutes to the Pro Football Hall of Fame Enshrinement Dinner. We had the honor of hosting one of the rooms. My husband offered the prayer and

I was the room host. This is something both of us enjoy. We meet great people and are given an opportunity to interact with some of the former football hall of famers.

While I had headaches and many nights did not sleep, I found that it was much better for me to be as active as possible so I would not give in to defeat of these ailments. Because of these problems, my prayer life definitely increased. This was a time for me to take stock of my life—where I was and where I needed to be in my relationship with God.

My husband was with me every step of the way, but I was beginning to feel as if I was a burden. Many nights he did not sleep because I did not sleep. He would sit up with me, hold me when the pain became unbearable, and always say, "God, you get the Glory out of what my wife is going through." My husband has always been one to pray throughout the night and this was very comforting to me.

My family was not used to me being sick, so they were very concerned. My Mother, at the time 88, would call me every day to see how I was feeling. All of my sisters and my children would call on a regular basis. I was not used to this kind of attention, but it was comforting to know that they were concerned and praying for me. My baby sister, Judy, was constantly doing research on the Internet trying to find some answers as to why I was not able to sleep.

In addition to my family, I had prayer warriors from Jesus Speaks Christian Center, my husband's church and my Chicago church, the Apostolic Church of God, praying, calling and e-mailing me.

One of my extended Chicago families is the Lee family and Mom Lee would call, chat for a few minutes and say, "Betty, we're praying for you."

Doctor E prepared a formula that he said would be the same as my natural hormones. He called in the prescription and I had it filled. It cost $70 and Medicare would not pay for this. This was much more than the $25 I was paying for the Premarin. After ordering it, I decided I did not want to take it. I continued taking the Premarin three times a week. I received different instructions from doctors. Some would say take the Premarin and others would say do not take it??? The problem was I would have severe hot flashes if I didn't take it. Also, if I did not take it for more than three days, I would become extremely nervous.

Doctor E also prescribed 500 mg. of "no flush Niacin" three times a day; 600 mg. of Red Yeast Rice three times a day; and, 25 mg. of DHEA once daily. Because of some of the changes my body went through while taking some of the other prescribed medications, I was just not mentally ready to take on anything new, so I decided not to take them.

Doctor E was a kind and caring person. He told me to read the book "Breakthrough" by Suzanne Somers and it would give me insight on some of the challenges I was having.

The night of May 1st, I was able to go to bed without a lot of pain in my head and seemingly was sleeping quite well until I awakened around 5:00 a.m. My body was tingling from my feet all the way to my arms. I felt as if I was in twilight, half asleep and half awake. I could barely speak but remember telling my husband my body was shutting down. I did feel that if I could get out of the panic mode, I might have gone into a deep sleep, which might not have been so bad. However, I clung to my husband very tightly. After about an hour, I got out of the bed but was in a very weak state.

For approximately two hours, I felt as if I was going to "lose my mind" and be admitted to the "psych ward". This is the only way I know how to explain what was happening. I had to walk, talk to myself and do some serious praying. I'm not sure what brought this on but the night of this attack I had taken some Schisandra 9a Chinese Herb, which is supposed to be good for insomnia. Not sure if that is what triggered it.

I put an ice pack on the back of my neck and was eventually able to fall asleep. This was the first time I can ever recall having a "panic attack". I had a good night's sleep. Thank God for the **BLESSING in the Midst of my Pain**!

The tingling sensation repeated itself again and again and happened most of the time when I was without sleep for three or four nights. It always felt as if my body was sleeping, but my head could not sleep. This is the only way I know how to describe the feeling. When I closed my eyes, they would flutter, but I could not sleep. Because I was so tired, my legs would become very heavy and I was unable to move them or any part of my lower body. As described above, my speech would slur. I was also super-sensitive to noise. It even hurt my ears when my husband brushed his teeth.

When this condition would come over me, the only way I could return to my normal state was to be left alone in a room by myself without any type of noise. It would take approximately five hours before I was able to move my legs. What a nightmare!

Whenever I would describe this to my primary care physician or any other doctor, including the ER, they would all say the same thing, "I have never heard of anything like this!" I remember one incident in June when this happened and I was finally able to at least speak. I asked my sister-in-law to take me to the hospital so they could better understand my condition. My husband was at the gym and I did not want to disturb him.

After the ER assigned me to a room, I explained to the doctor what was happening and how my legs were still partially, what seemed to be, paralyzed. The doctor told me that they are not equipped to handle anything like this in the ER. He said, "We are only able to handle life-threatening emergencies such as a heart attack!" Wow, I did not realize this. No wonder they would only prescribe some kind of medicine or give me a shot of morphine and send me home. Lesson learned—no more ER for me unless it is "life-threatening" or the pain becomes so intense I need strong medication. I pray this never happens!

The pressure in my head sometimes affects my vision causing me to take my glasses off for a short period of time to re-focus. I went to the eye doctor for a check-up to make sure there was nothing seriously wrong with my eyes. There were no changes. Praise God!

The pain in my head becomes somewhat unbearable when it reaches my forehead above my eyebrows. The pressure is so intense I feel as if a panic attack is beginning to happen. I must talk to myself and do a lot of praying to keep from flipping out. As I began to talk to others about my headaches and inability to sleep, I was simply amazed at the number that could relate because they were going through something similar. Most of them had headaches and more than half of them had problems sleeping. At least 1/3 of the ones I spoke with had the symptoms of "Occipital Neuralgia," but they had never had the diagnosis.

At 7:02 p.m. on Monday, May 22, 2009, I was feeling very sick to my stomach and weak. The pressure in my head became so intense it made me feel as if I was going to pass out. I had to place my hand on my head and apply pressure to stop the pain. After an hour, the pain subsided.

In a search for an answer to my pain, I ordered books on Shiatsu and the Bowen Technique. I shared the book with my physical therapist and my massotherapist. I get a massage every three weeks.

As if I did not have enough going on, my primary care physician recommended that I have my colonoscopy repeated. The doctor that had performed one approximately eight months ago had his licensed revoked because of being addicted to Vicodin. I was not mentally ready for this but had it performed. Everything was fine.

The lack of sleep was having serious effects on my body. I had no energy and bags under my eyes. It became more and more difficult for me to function during the day. However, I kept pushing myself and drinking coffee to keep me somewhat awake and alert.

Still searching for answers, I was able to find a wonderful support group on the Internet—MDJunction. This was truly an **UNEXPECTED BLESSING in the Midst of my Pain**! I found a group of men and women that had the same diagnosis as me—Occipital Neuralgia. We refer to this as "ON"! Unfortunately, there are teenagers with the same diagnosis and their parents are on the support line in search of answers and friendly folk that understand. I became such a regular person in this group and consistently responded to those reaching out that I was asked to be one of the group leaders. One thing I always share with them is my faith in God. I also tell them that in spite of their pain and what they are experiencing never stop believing or praying.

My husband would always pray for me, hold me and tell me, "We're in this together. I'm right here." That is always so comforting. Some of the women on my support line told me that their spouse was either not understanding or left them because of their health issues. If you have health issues and a supportive mate, don't take him/her for granted even though the wedding vows say "in sickness and in health." Appreciate your mate and pray for him/her. Some of them do not have the faith, patience or understanding so they walk away.

You always think you are in severe pain or having serious challenges until you talk to someone who is going through so much more. I found this on the support line. While many of these wonderful people have ON, some of them also have other complications. Some have had decompression surgery, RFA, that I described earlier, and many other treatments. For the majority of them, nothing has stopped their pain.

Some of those in my support group are taking 3 to 15 kinds of medication and are still in pain. The men and women are discouraged and disgusted because they feel the doctors they are seeing do not have an answer for what is causing their pain.

Some of them expressed they are of the opinion that the doctors have little or no interest in their well-being. It is if they are non-existent. I, too, experienced this with several of the many doctors that treated me. There were many times when I felt rushed and was just handed a prescription "to try" that might ease or eliminate my pain. Nothing worked!

I have met a lot of wonderful people on this support line and we continue to get new men and women every day. A lot of those that log on are searching for answers as to what is causing their pain since their doctors do not know. The newcomers describe their pain and then ask, "Do you think I might have ON?" One of the men in the group commented that he would rather have cancer; at least they would know how to treat it!

In the early part of June, after not being able to sleep for three nights, I asked my primary care physician to prescribe 110 mg. of Visatril. During one of my previous visits to the ER, I was given this medication and it allowed me to sleep for six hours. My primary care physician had her nurse inform me that the she could not prescribe this large dosage. I tried a smaller dosage, but it was not effective. The headaches continued and I could only sleep three or four hours every three days.

After three weeks of this sleeping pattern, I experienced what I called the "heavy leg syndrome" that I described in an earlier chapter. The last time this happened, I told my husband I just could not go through five hours of lying in the bed until my body would come back to life. So, I dragged myself out of bed in total pain, kept massaging my legs, walked out the back door into the yard until my body began to relax. The only problem was that I was simply exhausted. I began to cry and talk to God. My husband put his arms around me and let me know that in spite of what I was going through, God was with me. While sometimes my faith would grow a little weak, I always remembered the scripture telling me that God would never leave nor forsake me. This was truly a test of my FAITH! I cried out, "God where are you?"

The next day my husband received a telephone call from our friend Bishop Leon Wilson from Maryland. He said, "Pastor Mark, last night the Lord told me to pray for your wife." My husband began to tell him about my diagnosis. Bishop Wilson said he didn't know I was ill but he was obedient and prayed for me. (You never know who God has standing in the gap on your behalf. That is why it is important that when God puts someone on your heart, you should immediately pray.)

Because of not being able to sleep, my primary care physician referred me to a sleep doctor, who I will refer to as "Doctor G". My appointment was set for June 24th. I explained in detail my inability to sleep. His initial response was, "Well, I really don't know why you are not sleeping, but let's try a few things. First, I want to set you up with a sleep test to see if you have sleep apnea." Now this surprised me. How could I have sleep apnea when I couldn't sleep? However, at this point I was so in need of a good night's sleep that I was willing to try almost anything.

Doctor G then wrote a prescription for sleeping pills, 3 mg of Lunesta and 30 mg of Cymbalta. After not having slept for three nights, I filled the prescription. I slept for four hours. Hooray! The next night and several nights thereafter, I only slept two hours and then was unable to return to sleep.

The first time I took the Cymbalta I felt extremely nervous and was a little disoriented. This is probably some of the side effects, but I was just not able to handle it so I did not take another pill.

The first three weeks in June I was still struggling with insomnia. I went to the ER three times. Once I was given Morphine, another time 100 mg. of Visatril. The Visatril allowed me sleep for six hours. That was super! Another time I was given Morphine with Benadryl. When you have not slept in a long period of time and have severe pain, you will settle for almost anything to give you relief. I think this is how a lot of people become addicted. I did not want to become addicted to any kind of medicine, so I told myself that unless my pain was unbearable, I would not have any further injections of Morphine.

After one of my periods of not sleeping for three days and going into the "sleepy" leg syndrome, I was simply exhausted. It was very difficult for me to function. I went to my lounge chair and sat lifeless. My doorbell rang and it was my friend, Linda Brunk, a nurse from Aultman Hospital. I slowly moved to the door and when it opened, Linda, with a frightened look on her face, said, "Hi Betty just thought I would stop by and check on you." I could see the shocked look on her face as she saw me turn around and slowly return to my lounge chair.

She couldn't believe this was the vibrant, up-beat "Betty Mac" looking sad and bewildered and reclining in a lounge chair. Linda said, "Oh, my God, I didn't realize you were this sick. I can't believe what I'm seeing." I asked her not to tell anyone about my condition.

I was so glad to have company, even though I would never have called anyone to visit with me. I would have scared them half to death! Linda is such a caring and sincere person.

While still enduring the pain and with little or no sleep, I was trying to continue with some of my MDS projects. The board and I had been meeting on a weekly basis to discuss a search for an Executive Director. After several interviews, we came to a unanimous decision to offer the position to Terrance L. Jones, a very talented, intelligent young man from Canton.

Terrance was invited to meet with the Board to discuss the decision. At first, he was a little hesitant when offered the position. However, after asking questions and hearing from the Board, he stated that it would be an honor to serve as the next Executive Director of MDS. During the initial stages he would be interim, but the Board was confident that he would become the Executive Director.

Terrance was phasing out of another position but agreed to work part-time until my official retirement in September. I told Terrance that God would see him through any difficult situation as long as his faith remained strong. One thing I know for sure is that if you trust and never doubt, God will bring you out of any situation no matter how difficult.

Terrance is a young man I met several years after moving to Canton. I was chairing the first African-American Festival and was in need of talent. Several committee members advised me to contact Terrance. He had an annual Martin Luther King Talent Show and had access to a lot of great, young talent.

I left Terrance several messages but, unfortunately I was not able to make contact. I actually did not meet him until the following year. We often joke about this.

After our initial meeting and learning more about his talent show, I invited him to be a guest on my Canton City Schools TV show, "On Track with Betty Mac". I remember during the interview listening to his candid and sincere answers to my questions. I said to him, "I see greatness in you." This is a statement that a friend of mine, Les Brown, uses and I found it very appropriate to say to Terrance.

Terrance gave me a smile and said "Thank you Ms Betty." After that Terrance and I became good friends.

Terrance also became one of my faithful volunteers. At times it took a bit of arm twisting, but he always came through. He has a natural gift for working with youth. He is stern and commands respect. Guess what? They respect him.

In addition to working with MDS, I was still chairing the Hall of Fame Enshrinement Festival's Fashion Show. It was time for store fittings and important that I attend as many as possible. This is something I truly loved, having worked with Glory Productions, a modeling troupe in Chicago. I was very honored and felt **Blessed.**

Even though in pain, I was able to conduct the monthly meetings and fulfill my obligations as Chairman.

THE PAIN DOES NOT GO AWAY

I continued searching for something that would stop my headaches. My primary care physician stated she did not want me to have any more tests. She commented that every test comes back negative. My blood count was normal and there was nothing negative on my MRI or CT's. She told me that other than my headaches and inability to sleep, there was nothing wrong. She concluded by saying, "I really can't help you. I do not know what to do to help you sleep or stop the headaches."

I had asked her on several occasions if she could just put me in the hospital so they could observe me and perhaps be able to find an answer. She explained this was not possible. I recall one morning my husband drove me to her office. I had not slept for three nights, was totally exhausted to the point where I was actually incoherent, had slurred speech, and was as weak and limp as a dish rag. He explained my symptoms since, at this point, I was unable to speak. She very sympathetically explained there was nothing she could do and we left.

The pain intensified, so I asked my husband to once again take me to the ER. I had earlier said no more Morphine, but I was so tired, in pain, and sleepy that I took another injection. It relieved my pain, but I was still not able to sleep. I left the office somewhat angry, disappointed and wondering how many others, like me, were walking around in pain and unable to get an answer from a Doctor.

The headaches continued so I asked my primary care physician if she could schedule another MRI. At this time she did not feel it was necessary. Determined to get another MRI, I contacted my doctor at the Cleveland Clinic, the one that gave me the diagnosis of Occipital Neuralgia. After explaining how my pain had worsened, he requested another MRI.

On the day of the scheduled MRI, my husband drove me to the facility. When it was time for me to be placed into the machine for the MRI, I immediately pushed the little ball that was given to me in case I needed help. The lady administering the test moved me out of the machine to find out what I needed. I told her the machine appeared to be broken because there was a "loud" noise inside. She looked at me with a disgusting lift of her eyebrow and with a firm tone in her voice said, "There is always noise in the machine!" I commented that this was the fourth time in my life having an MRI and I had never heard a noise! I then told her that I was not able to endure the noise and would call later to re-schedule.

After calling my sister and a few friends that I knew had MRI's, I was told there is a noise, but if you are given a mild sedative you probably did not hear it. Wow, was I embarrassed. They were right. In the past I was given a pill before, but because I didn't want any kind of medication this particular time, I did not take anything. The noise was simply "nerve wracking!" Later, I did take the MRI and gritted my teeth and prayed until it was over!

I was becoming more and more concerned about my inability to sleep and was now focusing on a retreat that was on my schedule for July. This retreat, that I had been looking forward to for the past eight months, was sponsored by one of the Women's Organizations, Mind, Body and Soul at my former church, the Apostolic Church of God. The title of the retreat was SPA (Spiritual, Personal Adjustment). I was scheduled to conduct an early morning stretch and tone exercise class and during breakfast speak on healthy lifestyles. This was the second year I had been asked to be one of the presenters.

My sister Judy continued to assist me in trying to locate a specialist that might be able to help with my inability to sleep. She would send me new information every week.

The head pain was so severe; I was no longer able to sleep in my bed so I would recline in my lounge chair. When I was extremely exhausted, after not having slept for two or three nights, I would fall asleep for several hours in the chair. This was just not a good thing and my body was getting weaker and weaker.

On July 1st, my sister Judy sent me a link to the Chicago Northwestern University website. I read an article describing some of the research that was being done relating to sleep disorders. I sent an email to the person that wrote the article. Only as God would have it, within a few days I received a response giving me a phone number and the name, Dr. Phyllis Zee, a doctor in the Neurology Department.

On July 5th, I made a telephone call and inquired about an appointment with Dr. Zee. I was told that she travels quite a bit and only sees clients on Fridays. She continued by saying that Dr. Zee recently indicated she would see a few more new clients as her schedule would permit. I was then referred to another operator. I briefly explained my situation and pleaded with the operator to do whatever was possible to get me an appointment. I was placed on hold. When the operator returned, he said, "Can you come on Friday the 10th." I immediately said, "YES." Again, as God would have it, I was scheduled to be at the Apostolic Church of God's Women's Retreat that very weekend!

I called my sister-in-law Frances, who was traveling with me to the retreat, to see if she was able to go one day early. My appointment was at 10:00 a.m. on Friday, so I needed to leave on Thursday. Frances was able to travel with me on Thursday.

MY TRIP TO CHICAGO

Thursday morning, July 9th, Frances and I drove to Chicago. That evening, I was unable to sleep. At 5:30 a.m. I awakened Frances and told her that I needed to get dressed and get out of the house. We were staying with my girlfriend Bobbi. I was very nervous, my skin began to itch, and I was fighting a panic attack. Frances began to pray and I jumped into the shower, which gave me a little relief. At 7:00 a.m. we headed downtown and parked in the Northwestern parking lot. Since we had a lot of time before my 10:00 a.m. appointment, we had breakfast at a lovely outdoor café. I drank a large cup of coffee to keep myself awake. After we had a light breakfast, I told my sister-in-law that I would like to walk to Catholic Charities where a good friend of mine, Christene Dykes-Sorrell, was employed. Christene was one of the young ladies I hired 39 years ago when I was an employee at Catholic Charities. My sister-in-law does not like to walk but she knew I needed to be kept busy until it was time for my appointment, so she readily agreed.

Upon arrival, we were informed that Mrs. Sorrell was in a meeting but would be free within 30 minutes. The staff person was kind enough to allow us to wait. When Christene arrived, we were greeted with a hello and a warm hug. She then escorted us into her office. We had a wonderful visit as she shared with us some delightful stories about her emergency services program. We did a little reminiscing and shared some laughs. I remembered that she was a praying woman and upon leaving, I asked that she pray for me. When she said "Amen," I felt re-energized, gave her a hug, and Frances and I left.

The visit and walk back to Northwestern University was perfect timing for my appointment with Dr. Zee. I was introduced to one of Dr. Zee's assistants who gave me paperwork to complete. After completing the paperwork and answering many questions, Dr. Zee walked in and greeted me. She was a tiny, bubbly person with a genuine warm smile that completely relaxed me.

She wanted to know who referred me. When I told her I found her on the Internet and was able to get an appointment, she looked at me with a puzzled look and then shook her head and smiled. I was hoping that she was thinking it had to be God.

I had brought a notebook with documented information about my headaches and sleepless nights. While I was meeting with her assistant, Dr. Zee had an opportunity to review the material. She commented that she noticed I do not like taking medication and, therefore, would keep that in mind when she made decisions on my treatment. Wow, this made me feel good. Her next statement was, "I'm sure we'll be able to help you sleep." Now I was ecstatic. I finally found a doctor that did not say she didn't know why I was not sleeping or who just prescribed sleeping pills.

After answering a few questions, she said, "You need to be 're-programmed'. Your sleeping pattern is completely off because of your headaches, sitting up sleeping on the sofa and then trying to sleep in a lounge chair." She then gave me a treatment plan. "I want you to go to bed at your regular time, whatever you choose that to be—10:00, 11:30 or even 12 midnight. If you are not asleep within 20 or 30 minutes, get up, sit in a chair, do not lean back in a sleeping position, do relaxation therapy, and then return to bed. Try this off and on for several hours. If after 3 or 4 a.m. you are not able to sleep, no matter how tired, I want you to get out of the bed and do not attempt to sleep until the next evening. Even if you become sleepy during the day, do not go to sleep until evening."

The next part of the treatment I was to spend three hours outside every day that the sun was shining and exercise for one hour a day until I perspired. She further indicated that I was to exercise even if my head was hurting! Wow! That was a tall order but I was ready for the challenge.

Next, she prescribed "Cognitive Behavior Therapy!" She asked that I make an appointment with another neurologist in her department, "Doctor H".

I then told Dr. Zee about the pain in my legs and how my body would shut down after not being able to sleep for three or four days. She had not heard of anything like this but suggested I try Neurotin. You guessed it; I did not take this medication.

The next thing she did was give me a sleep log that I was to complete and fax back to her office every ten days.

I gave her a big hug and thanked her for her kindness and caring spirit. I then met with the receptionist to schedule an appointment with Doctor H. Thank God the doctor was able to see me that following Wednesday while I would still be in the Chicago area.

APOSTOLIC CHURCH OF GOD—MIND, BODY, SOUL (SPIRITUAL PERSONAL ADJUSTMENT (SPA) RETREAT)

If you've never experienced the anointing and God working through others, you might not fully understand this portion of the book.

After my meeting with Dr. Zee, my sister-in-law and I drove to Galena, Illinois for the retreat. It was a three-hour drive and I was feeling pretty good. I had a very large cup of coffee to keep me going, so I drove the entire time without tiring or experiencing any pain.

Upon arrival at the retreat, we were warmly greeted by Janice Dortch and some of her staff. Jan, in her very jovial way said, "Hi Betty and Frances, you are just in time to eat." The meal was simply delicious. They seated me at a table with some folks I knew and some I didn't. While sitting there, something appeared to be flying in front of me. I did not know what it was and I began to fan my hand to move it from me. Sitting two seats from me a very attractive, tiny lady looked and beckoned for me to come to her. I went over and she asked me what I was fanning. I told her I did not know. She said it was a butterfly. I asked, "What does that mean?" She said, "You are going to release something!" The theme of the retreat was "Release". I thanked her and went back to my seat.

When I returned to my seat I inquired about the lady that had just spoken to me. I was told, "Her name is Prophetess Haddon and she is a dynamic woman of God."

Shortly after I finished eating, the program began and Prophetess Haddon was called upon for remarks. She opened by saying, "I did not know that your theme for the evening was about butterflies, but I saw one on this lady right here," and she pointed to me. As she looked at me and continued her remarks, I felt the power of God come over me and I fell prostrate on the ground. Wow, that was an awesome experience. I can remember lying there and felt a warm, calmingly sensation enter my body. I remained on the ground for a few minutes and very slowly came to my feet. I looked around and saw the women who were all dressed in white praising God and enjoying the presence of the Holy Spirit.

That evening, even though I was relaxed and calm, I had a difficult time sleeping and was concerned about how I would feel the next morning when I was scheduled to conduct the "morning stretch and tone" class at 8:00 and a workshop during breakfast. I tossed and turned and finally fell asleep, only to wake up two hours later. I lie awake the rest of the night talking to God.

The next morning I was tired but determined to perform my duties. When I began my exercise class I felt renewed and began to talk to the women about the importance of stretching to prevent injuries and help relieve various types of body pain and stress.

My lecture at breakfast, in addition to talking about a healthy lifestyle, centered on my diagnosis of "Occipital Neuralgia" and my difficulty sleeping. I also spoke about how I felt that my pain was a direct result of the many hours on the computer. After my presentation, many women came to me indicating their inability to sleep and how some of them were experiencing the same kind of head pain. I was simply amazed at how many women were suffering with some of the same symptoms but had not been diagnosed. They were prescribed pain pills for temporary relief.

The Friday evening service had a dynamic speaker from Springfield, Ohio, Evangelist Anne Story Pratt. She indicated that God was taking her in a different direction than what she had originally planned. She began to motion for different women to come forward and would then give them a word of prophecy. My head was bowed and when I raised it, the speaker was pointing her finger and motioned for me to come forward. When I walked up to her she said, "You have been going from one thing to another in your body." She then placed her hands on me and I once again found myself on the ground under the anointing! I heard her say, "Pick her up!" I felt someone's arms around me as I stood to my feet. The speaker came from the platform, put her arms around me and said, "We're going to walk this off." Evangelist Pratt walked me up and down in front of the room three times. When I returned to my seat I began to "dance in the spirit." I would estimate this lasted for approximately 15 minutes or more.

Before I was called to the front, I had said to my sister-in-law, "I'm so very, very tired. I can hardly keep my eyes open." Well when the anointing hits, you become energized.

That night I slept 5 ½ hours; the most I had slept in quite some time.

The Wednesday after the retreat, I met with Doctor H, the neurologist in Dr. Zee's office. After reviewing all of my information, Doctor H was not convinced that I had "Occipital Neuralgia." She suggested I have an angiogram of the neck to look for vertebrae and carotid artery dissection. Because of the pain I have in my legs, she wanted me to have an ESR blood test. The ESR blood test is an important tool that helps doctors diagnose conditions that can cause inflammation, pain, and other symptoms.

I was very pleased with my visit to Chicago and returned to Canton with my spirits uplifted and feeling very energized and encouraged that things were going to get better.

By keeping daily health logs, I discovered some of the "triggers for my headaches.

The following things definitely cause me pain: too much sugar, overeating, stress, walking more than four miles at a time, more than two meetings in one day, including lunch with a friend; consistent appointments before 10 a.m. that require me to rush to get things accomplished and if I am on the computer for more than one hour at a time.

RESULTS OF MY VISIT WITH DR. ZEE

Upon returning to Canton, I made an appointment with my primary care physician and discussed my visit to Chicago with Dr. Zee and Doctor H. She was very pleased with the results. We both agreed that I did not need to have any additional testing as recommended by Doctor H.

Every day the sun was out, I spent up to three hours outdoors. I started my exercise routine and scheduled an appointment with Dr. Wilcox for my "Cognitive Behavior Therapy." After two weeks of this routine, I began sleeping three to four hours a night. I would fax my sleep logs to Dr. Zee's office every ten days and within five days someone from her office would call and give me feedback. I was simply amazed at the support and care I received from Dr. Zee's office. The young lady that called was always so polite, kind and caring. With each log there would be different instructions to aid with my sleeping condition.

I remember one time after faxing my logs; one of Dr. Zee's staff called informing me that Dr. Zee was out of the country but would get back to me as soon as she returned. What a **Blessing.**

We have a lot of great and caring doctors in this country and I'm sure they exceed those that are not. It is my opinion that those that are not need to either live up to their oath of giving the best care possible to clients or find another profession. I feel they are giving the industry a bad reputation.

I continued Dr. Zee's treatment plan and in my sixth week, I began to sleep five and six hours each night. Never take sleep for granted. If you are able to sleep, you are BLESSED! I suggest that you not rely on sleeping pills, but try to find the cause for your inability to sleep. Are you stressed? Is it your diet? Do some research on your own. Get on the Internet and don't settle for one person's opinion. Most of all PRAY and ask God for guidance. Get in touch with your body. No one knows it better than God and you.

My sleeping definitely improved but my headaches continued. My pain was worse at night. The most severe pain was behind my left ear on the lesser occipital nerve. I would use hot and cold compresses, apply pressure with my fingers, and PRAY. After three or four hours, it would go away.

With Occipital Neuralgia you never know what to expect. Some days my head throbs, other days it feels as if it is in a pressure cooker, and yet on other days the pain is in the top of my head close to the area that is referred to as neuralgia and headache pain or sometimes the pain is in the front of my face like a sinus headache.

When the headaches appear at night, many times I'm unable to place my head on the pillow and force me to sit up until the pain subsides. At times I try a rolled up large towel and place it under my neck. Another thing I try is a cervical pillow that can be placed in the freezer. I try one of these treatments until I find something that works.

STILL WORKING IN SPITE OF MY PAIN

I had the Fashion Show behind me but needed to fulfill two more commitments.

Maria, owner of Arcadia Grill in downtown Canton, is someone that genuinely cares about the needy and always tells me, "Betty, it's all about the babies. We must do whatever we can to take care of them." If you say,

"My agency needs," before you finish the sentence she will say, "What can I do to help?" And, she helps everyone!

Every year Maria has "Christmas in July" and proceeds benefit agencies such as MDS, Domestic Violence Shelter, Community Services and the list is endless. She doesn't just do this in July, Maria has so many signs on her door for things she supports, you can't see inside her restaurant.

This year, because of my headaches, I was not able to stay for the entire event. Maria, who has breast cancer, seems to never miss a beat. She told me to go home and she would make sure our event was successful. What can you say about a person like Maria? She's definitely one of a kind!

My final commitment was to the Annual O'Jays Weekend that was scheduled for August 15-17 in Canton. I was responsible for the local PR. This is always a fun event and I enjoy working with the committee and interacting with the O'Jays.

The night before the major concert, that featured Frankie Beverly and Maze, The Whispers, and the O'Jays, I had a serious headache and was only able to sleep two hours. My videographer and I were scheduled to cover the entire event, which included setting up the stage, the "Love Train" ride with Eddie, capturing the crowd as they gathered for the event, and interviewing some of the committee members and guests. My prayer was, "Dear Lord, please help me get through this last major event." I was full of coffee and re-energized from being in the sun that was truly bright and hot, 90 degrees. I had a wonderful time interacting with some awesome people, not only from Canton but from D.C., L.A., New York, Illinois and many other cities and states. We had a record crowd of 23,000 plus at Fawcett Stadium.

The next day, I covered the O'Jays Parade on O'Jays Boulevard and the Family Reunion in Nimisilla Park. Monday morning we were at the historical William Powell Golf Course and that evening we met at the Pro Football Hall of Fame for the O'Jays Scholarship Banquet. I was blessed to interview HB Barnum a living legend in the music business, as a producer, songwriter, arranger and conductor for the biggest stars in history, including, Elvis, Sinatra, All the "Motown" stars, Lou Rawls etc. & musical director for Aretha Franklin for 35 years.

Whew! I was definitely getting my three hours of sunshine and more than an hour of daily exercise. While I enjoyed each event, I was truly glad when this weekend was over. I had little or no sleep, but God was with me and helped me fulfill my commitment.

Now that the O'Jays weekend was over, I began to concentrate on my Retirement Party and the 10th Year Anniversary of Multi-Development Services of Stark County.

I was only going into the office one day a week and doing some work from home. Terrance was beginning to settle into the position and would call me when he had questions.

The MDS Board consists of some wonderful and dedicated folks. The President of MDS, Rod Meadows of Motter & Meadows Architects, a generous, kind and caring person, has been an avid supporter of MDS for the past five years. His concern for the agency and clients we serve is typical of his personality and character. Charleen Davidson, MDS Vice-President and one of the Assistant Vice-Presidents of Consumer Banking, has supported MDS since its inception. When I was unable to get a line of credit, it was Charleen, who at that time was with Unizan Bank, who stepped out and said, "Don't worry Betty, we'll give you a line of credit." And, Praise God they did.

Janet Haldeman, MDS Secretary and a resident of the Summit neighborhood, has been faithful for the past seven years. She loved working with the youth making bears, quilts and other items. Her family has lived in the Summit neighborhood for more than 35 years.

Louise Bishop, MDS Treasurer whom I call my prayer warrior, is always available to help in the office or at events. Her prayers have definitely helped carry us through some very difficult times. She has been faithful for the past six years.

As long as my head was not hurting, I was still available for the monthly neighborhood clean up programs with the SNET II youth. I loved the interaction with the volunteers and neighbors.

Terrance and Betty

MY RETIREMENT PARTY AND 10th YEAR ANNIVERSARY OF MULTI-DEVELOPMENT SERVICES OF STARK COUNTY

September 26, 2009 is a day I shall always remember. This was the 10th Year Anniversary celebration for the Agency I founded, Multi-Development Services of Stark County, and my retirement.

The Board and Terrance planned a very memorable occasion that started when a limousine arrived to transport my husband and me to the event. Now that was simply special. The evening was filled with singing, testimonials, and a slide presentation highlighting many of the MDS programs.

The big surprise came when I was presented with a "Golden Dove Award." For the past ten years, I would always present this award to others. Refer to the section on Golden Dove Awards.

In my 12 years of living in Canton, I have been presented with numerous awards that include the Canton Negro Old Timers Community Service Award, inducted into the Canton YWCA Women's Hall of Fame, Juneites Community Award, Deliverance Church Christian Hall of Fame, Beautiful People Award, Stark County Realtor's Association Community Award, Destiny Place Human Service Award and several others.

At the end of the celebration, I presented Terrance with a Bible and told him it was his "sword." I also told him that any and everything he needs is found in this wonderful book.

After the official ceremony, we had a lovely reception with good food and entertaining music provided by an MDS board member, Mia Macomson, referred to as Mia Morning.

During the month of October, I had two major attacks with pain behind my left ear. I remembered that I had a "pressure pump" and decided to use it. It definitely helped relieve the pain. For some reason, October 18th was the "best" pain-free day I had had in six months. I can't recall anything that I did that was different, but I gave God praise for the **BLESSED** day!

VITAMINS, HERBS, WATER AND COLONICS

Janet Hawkins, who has been my herbalist for eight years, is dedicated and concerned about people's health issues. In 2003, when I had severe stomach pain and had an endoscopy and barium test that showed no problems, I tried all kinds of medication that did not help. Janet solved the problem with olive leaf drops and aloe vera! During one of my visits, I asked her if she knew anyone that administered colonics, the infusion of liquid into the colon through a tube in the rectum. I refer to a colonic as another form of taking an enema but with greater results! Big smile! At that particular time, she did not have a resource. Several years later, she introduced me to Linda Clifton, Founder of Crossroads Education and Wellness.

Linda and I became good friends. She is another person that cares and is concerned about people. Linda is constantly researching and looking for ways to better our health.

Twice a year Linda invites Dr. Dona Garofano, a Certified Nutritional Consultant, Certified Naturopathic Doctor in New Jersey, Certified Master Herbalist and a Licensed Health Officer in New Jersey to visit Crossroads and administer a Dried Blood Cell Analysis for registered clients. She also gives a power-point presentation to educate women about a healthier way of living with supplements.

In October, I met with Dr. Garofano and was immediately impressed when I heard about her passion for helping women live a healthier lifestyle. She thoroughly explained to me that the DBA works by acquiring a sample of blood (with a small prick from the finger, which I voluntarily give her). She then views the sample through a high-powered microscope to determine the imbalances present in the body created by the specific patterns the blood makes. These patterns, which set-up from the droplets voluntarily sampled from me, show areas of stress, acidity, toxicity, hormonal imbalance and the like.

She made it clear that the DBA is not a diagnosis, but a screening tool to analyze the present conditions of the body and help access nutritional needs of clients.

After my DBA, Dr. Garofano targeted areas in my body that were out of balance. She made recommendations of supplements that would bring my body back into balance. The body heals itself and needs nutrition in order for the healing to take place.

In our discussion, she explained that the DBA is nothing new but was first introduced in Europe in 1920.

I informed her that I had been on Premarin for 28 years and had some doctors tell me to continue taking it and others said not to take it. One of Dr. Garofano's specialties is women's issues of hormonal, thyroid imbalances and adrenal stress that create symptoms such as depression, mood swings, weight gain, irritability and more. After she explained to me the dangers of Premarin, I decided to discontinue taking it. I now use Pure Gest Progesterone crème and it is working fine.

If you would like more information about Dr. Garofano, please log on to her website at www.greathallsofhealing.com

I remember several months earlier, Linda and Janet talked to me about a Japanese water product. This water is produced in your home when simple tap water has been filtered, then restricted through ionization.

When I first tasted the water, I drank less than half a glass, it made me extremely dizzy. I was told this was the 9.5 pH and I would need to start on the lower pH, which was 7.5. Both of these ladies suggested that I make a conscious effort to stay on the water for a longer period of time, believing that it would help my headaches and make me rest better at night.

During the month of November, I continued with my program of exercise, watching my diet, limiting my time on the computer and making it a practice of not doing anything before 10:00 in the morning. Wow, just not having to get up and rush to the office was a **BLESSING**!

On Christmas, I was sitting at dinner with my husband and giving thanks and praise to God for a wonderful day. This time last year I was in the ER and they gave me a shot of Morphine to get me through the day. God is truly a good God!

For the past six years, I had been taking medicine for my bladder. I decided to stop taking the medicine to see if it was really helping. Well, I didn't feel any better or worse, so I did not return to taking the medication. I made more of a concerted effort to watch my diet, drink cranberry juice, and do my kegel exercises. Kegel are exercises to increase muscle strength and elasticity in the female pelvis. Ladies, if you haven't tried cranberry juice and kegel exercises, I suggest you at least try. These are also preventative things for bladder problems. Oh, it pays to research!

THE PAIN RETURNS

In the middle of January, I wanted to know if the water was helping so I decided not to drink it for two weeks. Four days after not drinking the water my head began throbbing so profusely that I became disoriented and could barely speak. My husband had to hold me to keep me from going into a serious "panic attack!"

He began to pray and ask God to intervene. I fell into a deep sleep and slept for about six hours. When I awoke my head once again started pounding. I could not figure out what was happening and why the pain had returned.

The pain in my right arm, that I had problems with as a result of the herniated C7 disk, also returned. It was so painful that I had to return to physical therapy. As if that was not enough, I began to have problems with pain in my right hip that went all the way down the side of my leg to my ankle. OH MY GOD what is happening to my body?

Now, what was this all about? Did this have something to do with the water? I didn't want to drink this water if I was going to be sick once I stopped drinking it. Now, I realize there are some medications that folks must take to function and I'm not knocking that, but I'm talking about my body and what works for me. I talked with several others that were drinking the water and they were not having any problems. In fact, they were feeling 100 percent better.

I think some of this was brought on by stress and worrying about the water! I had to really pray and talk to myself about fear knowing that perfect love casts out all fear. God, was my faith weakening? This kept me on my knees longer and communicating more with God.

I talked with several health practitioners that had the water. One of them told me the water was numbing my body so I did not feel the pain and once I stopped drinking it, the pain returned. The other person told me that my body was too sick to drink the water and I should only drink a small amount each day. Well, I decided to mix the water with one of my favorite bottled waters. This worked. It took about a week before I started feeling better. My headaches were less frequent and I was able to sleep at least 5 or 6 hours a night.

My prayer time and soul-searching made me realize that because I was feeling better, I had begun working long hours at home on several projects and staying on the computer for two and three hours at a time. Wow, I can't believe I was actually doing this after going through such pain just a year ago. How soon we forget where God has brought us, only to sometimes revert back to the original problem! Okay God, you have my attention. I am going to slow down, log the amount of time I spend on the computer and learn how to REST!

Still in search for answers to many questions about my headaches and a possible cure for occipital neuralgia, Dr. Prowell told me I needed to find a Neuromuscular Therapist in my area since I was not able to come to Chicago as often as he needed to see me. I did an online search and, as God would have it, I found a gentleman named Michael Dallas Jones whose office was within 15 minutes from where I live. I clicked on his website at *www.fibromyalgiafullresolution.com.* Wow, what a story about this triathlete's life. I recommend that you read how he had to take charge of his body.

Michael treats all areas of the body including cranial sacral therapy and visceral (organ) massage. He has taken the St. Johns neuromuscular seminars. Additionally, he teaches those he treats to know how to do self-massage and techniques to know how not to over-extend themselves according to their condition.

I sent an email and several days later he responded and asked that I call him. Wow, Michael loves to talk and share. After being on the phone for about 45 minutes, we ended the conversation with a day and time for the two of us to meet.

The following week, I met with Michael. We became instant friends! He had some very informative videos for me to watch that were made in 1991 at the St. John Neuromuscular Pain Relief Institute in Largo, Florida. He also put me in touch with Dr. Leonard Knell, a retired Orthopedic Surgeon with 34 years of practice in Canton, OH, who validates Michael's treatment of Fibromyalgia and Occipital Neuralgia.

I discussed my book with Mike (that's what I call him) and told him I was completing the final chapter of my book and would like to meet with him for a statement on his practice. Mike also has a partner named Ross A. Carter.

Mike and I set a meeting date for March 8th. Dr. Knell would also attend this meeting

February 4th my husband and I traveled to Logansport, Indiana to the homegoing services for my oldest brother Freddie.

When I returned to Canton, I immediately made my water mixture and drank my usual gallon of water and began to make more time in my day to rest. I began to regularly juice carrots, celery, green peppers and apples as well as watch my intake of sugar and starch. I was feeling better.

I discussed this with Mike and he suggested, until he has time to set up my treatment plan and get to the root cause of my headaches and intense pain, to continue to only drink my bottled water.

While talking to God during one of my daily prayers, I so clearly heard him tell me that this was my time to do things that I enjoy, rest and focus on completing my book. After he spoke this to me, I felt a peace and calmness that I had not felt in some time. It was such a wonderful feeling. I hated to move from the spot where I was praying wanting this feeling to last forever.

I recall other times in my life when I had become so involved in my work, not resting or eating properly and God would "zap" me with fatigue, sometimes a headache or other things that required me to rest for a few days. One time in particular, I went to visit Mattie, a friend of mine in Chillicothe, OH. Her daughter Linda picked me up from the airport in Columbus. I slept all the way from the airport (30 minutes) to her home. When I arrived at Linda's, I sat on the sofa and slept another hour.

She allowed me to sleep and awakened me when it was time for her to take me to her mother in Chillicothe. After I arrived in Chillicothe, greeted Mattie and her husband, I asked her if I could go straight to bed. I had no idea I was this exhausted. It was approximately 9 p.m. and I slept until noon the next day. Mattie woke me to eat and after eating, I went back to bed. I slept off and on for three days! It's amazing that I was working so hard I didn't realize how fatigued I was. This is not a good thing BUT, I still didn't learn to get proper rest. I always put work and others first before taking care of me. I've had to learn the hard way, through occipital neuralgia, that you have to take care of your health first and foremost.

Back to my story.

One month later, March 5th, my husband and I once again traveled to Logansport but this time for a very happy occasion, the celebration of my Mother's 90th Birthday.

The night before the event, we had a decorating party and a birthday celebration for my nephew Jaylon. I had serious pain behind my right ear but did not want the family to know I was suffering so I smiled and interacted with them as if everything was fine. That night I was only able to sleep three hours. The next morning, even though I was very tired, I did a 30 minute workout on the treadmill. I began to feel better.

My Mother's Birthday Party was a spectacular event that brought many local and out of state friends and relatives together. My oldest sister Melba did an outstanding job planning this party and her daughter Terri wowed us with her unique decorating skills. My other two sisters Wanda and Judy added their support to make this a wonderful event. Dwayne Lee from Chicago was the guest soloist. Family members included mother's children, grandchildren, great grandchildren and one of her two great-great grandchildren.

March 8th I met with Mike and Dr. Knell. We chatted, shared and laughed for 90 minutes. I feel so blessed to have met and be in the company of these two wonderful gentlemen. I set a date for both of them to appear on my local cable TV show. It is my desire that someone watching my show will be enlightened, helped and learn more about "occipital neuralgia."

I am going to do more research and talk to others that are drinking the water to see what kind of results they are getting.

I know that in God's time, my headaches will be completely gone. He has the power to heal me or He can work through someone else. Either way, He is in control. Now, if I choose to continue working long hours, stay on the computer too long and other things that I know causes headaches, shame on me. God had to "break" me in order to "save" me! So, I am using what I'm experiencing to reach out and help others. I will do my best knowing that God will do the rest! By the way, my HDL is now 96 and my LDL is 199. This is without medication.

I continue to share with my friends on the MDJunction support line. These are truly a wonderful group of people with a sense of humor in spite of their pain. I shared that I do daily stretching exercises that help strengthen my neck and relieve my headache. Some of them asked that I share my tape, which I did. They are truly a **BLESSING in the Midst of my Pain**!

Comments from several of my online support group friends from MDJunction.

For the past sixteen months, I have been coping with a pain high up in my skull. When I first felt it, I thought it would take a simple trip to my doctor and physical therapist, and then it would be over. That, unfortunately, was not the case, and I trekked from acupuncture to chiropractic, and finally, to a neurologist, who diagnosed the condition as Occipital Neuralgia. He prescribed a regimen of pain pills that were to be increased weekly as I did the exercises he recommended. In a few weeks, I would be pain-free.

However, that did not happen, and I confess I was obstinate about taking that many pain meds. I next visited a cranial-sacral doctor, who was actually able to reach what I started calling "the evil spot in my head," and I felt temporary relief, but the pain came back.

Recently, I found someone who specializes in decompression therapy, and the pain seems to be lessening. He explained that what I was feeling was referred pain, and that the actual culprit is a herniated disc at my C #2 cervical vertebra in my neck. The result is a pinched nerve, which registers pain high up in my cranium. The decompression creates a vacuum between discs so that the disc material will stop impinging on the nerve and go back in place, thus relieving the pain. I have faith this will happen, but it will take many treatments. It is definitely worth it to me, and I look forward to being totally pain-free.

I felt quite alone with my problem. None of my friends or relatives knew anything about ON, so I went on line to search for others with this condition. I found quite a few wonderful people who are coping with various stages, from being bed-ridden for years, to having this a relatively short time and being able to function in life almost normally, like Betty Smith and me. All of us wanted to reach out, and we found each other. It helps to have kind words and encouragement from people who "have been there," and understand.

Mieke Tazelaar

Mieke is also an author and was kind enough to send me an autographed copy of her book "The Apple Eater."

This is a message from another one of my support line friends Chloe:

My ON hasn't changed and I am still on a waiting list for the wireless implant although now I am concerned about the infection risk with this. My neurologist said that he had heard of cases of meningitis after implant so I am going to avoid it for a bit. I am a bit let down as I was hoping the implant would be something that could help me take less meds. I just feel there is no hope at the moment for an ON cure . . . .

There is no way I would have the nerve decompression surgery, sorry, I don't want to sound negative about it, but know in my case that to have surgery where the problem could already be scar tissue just doesn't impress me.

So I am frustrated with the amount of meds I am taking but don't know what to do about it. I am just hanging in there. I would appreciate comments on this amount of meds.

Here is a list of meds I am taking daily at the moment. I can't believe that the neurologist just added two more.

Prilosec for (GERD)Gastrointestinal Reflux Disease, Basal Insultin Lantus for diabetes, Ammaryl, Metformin actos. These four keep my sugars between 80-120 after dealing with out of control sugars for a few years I am proud of this. I also take Neurotin, Prozac, and Vicodin. These three keep my ON spasms down from up to 300 per day to about 20 and keep the headache just bearable.

Lipitor for cholesterol which I can probably go off after next blood test . . .

Benazepril to help my kidneys I always forget this one so it has been hard to accept that a neurologist would add more meds.

The new meds are Zanaflex (muscle relaxer) and Oxcarbazepine which the neurologist claims is a new anti-seizure that would help calm the nerves and can be taken with Neurontin. Magnesium for muscle cramps. I just stopped Viokase pancreatic enzymes. This list just seems outrageous to me. I just can't drop my gerd or diabetic pills and need Prozac for my post traumatic stress so it doesn't leave much to stop.

On a more positive note. I am trying to sit in the sun for 30 minutes per day and 3 times per week I drag myself out to a long walk with the dogs in a sports field.

(In spite of all she is going through Chloe has a wonderful sense of humor.)

Another one of my support group friends—3/8/2010

Occipital Neuralgia; Cranial Neuralgia; Intractable Migraine; Chronic Daily Headaches; Tension Headaches; and the list goes on. It all means the same thing—pain . . . unrelenting pain . . . a constant unwanted companion . . . and the gradual loss of the ability to function "normally" as the ability to focus on complex tasks or issues slips away.

If this sounds like anything you're experiencing, take heart, and cling to your faith; it'll keep you from losing hope, and you may be surprised at the doors that will open when you least expect it.

For over 20 years, I've had a headache that simply refuses to part company with me. I received great relief from the occipital nerve decompression surgery that Neurologist Dr. Pamela Blake referred me to. It was performed by Dr. Carlton Perry. Both doctors are in Houston, Texas.

Unfortunately, the relief I experienced from the occipital nerve decompression was short lived as my frontal/trigeminal nerves really got angry a couple months after the procedure. Now six months after the frontal nerve decompression surgery, it's almost like I've taken a few steps backwards.

However, as my wife likes to say, when God closes a door, he always opens another one. A recent report from Dr. Bahman Guyuron covering patients over five years after surgery shows great promise. I know better than most how desperately we want a one stop shop; a fix that really fixes; something that will help us to stop wondering not if, but how bad tomorrow's headache will be. Until that happens, we just have to keep taking one day at a time, as God's Word says, and trust that He has plan for us, and that plan is not to suffer without hope. Things will get better, and hopefully we can help each other by showing our resilience each step of the way, and comforting each other as we endure something that I wouldn't wish on anyone.

I was surprised by how many people are enduring what I'm enduring, especially since my family (parents and sibling) does not understand my situation at all, and has even said that "it's all in my head." But I've been blessed with the most wonderful wife in the world, and two great children who constantly remind me how blessed I really am, and to not give up or give in to despair. Sometimes that's easier said than done, but it has to be done. I've received a great deal of help from my fellow sufferers, and I hope I've been able to help them as well.

So hang in there; there's work being done in this field every day, and advances are being made regularly. But mainly, don't worry about tomorrow, God's already been there!

Judson

MY DAILY ROUTINE

I try to be out of bed by 7:30 a.m. However, if I've had a difficult time sleeping the night before, I sometimes do not get up until 9:00. This is another reason I do not plan my day before 10:00 a.m. or later. Upon awaking, I bathe and put on my workout clothes. My next step is to drink 12 ounces of water with a teaspoon of apple cider vinegar and a teaspoon of honey. With this water I take my daily vitamin. I then mix a gallon of water in a jar with some freshly squeezed lemon juice and honey or Organic Maple Syrup. I pour half of this mixture into another jar and take it with me when I leave the house to make sure I get a sufficient amount of water during the day. I drink the remainder of the water before 7 p.m. There are also other vitamins I take that were suggested by Dr. Garofano.

I squeeze either oranges or grapefruit; sometimes I mix them, and place it in the refrigerator. I drink this about an hour after I finish my glass of vinegar water.

Some mornings I make a smoothie that consists of strawberries, blueberries, honey, protein powder, sometimes without the powder, fresh squeezed orange juice and ice cubes. This is a very filling and refreshing drink. If I don't drink a smoothie, I might have a bran muffin or oatmeal.

After my water routine, it is time for the most important part of my day, my prayer time with God.

After my prayer time, I work out for an hour on my treadmill, trampoline, and/or perform my version of a combination of Pilates and yoga. Every other day I use 5 pound weights. Some days I go to the local health club and workout or take a Pilates class. Wow, do I feel refreshed.

This routine takes about two hours. If you are working, you can have a similar routine, you just need to get up a little earlier. I would rather take time for this routine than spend time in the ER or take a lot of medication. Ask yourself, what would you rather do?

Some days I lunch with friends and other days I spend time at Timken, one of our local high schools, and work with students in the Broadcast Media Department. This is where I tape my "On Track with Betty Mac" TV show. My goal is "little or no stress!"

My evenings are spent preparing dinner for my husband or eating out, reading, writing and/or watching TV. We are both avid Cleveland Cavalier fans and rarely miss watching a game. LeBron James and other athletes are on my daily prayer list.

It is my desire to be a motivating force to help others that are suffering with Occipital Neuralgia, talk with men and women about the importance of waiting on God for a mate, and teach workshops about the benefits of "Taking care of your body, the Temple of the Holy Spirit."

My 12 years in Canton OH have been simply wonderful. I'm often asked by my friends in Chicago and Canton if I miss living in Chicago. My emphatic answer is always "NO"!

I can say that because I visit Chicago on a regular basis, at least six times a year. It is an easy drive or a little over an hour on an airplane. I live 10 minutes from the Akron-Canton Airport.

When I'm not visiting Chicago, my family and friends come to Canton. When in Chicago, I'm able to sit, chat and sometimes dine with my former Pastor and his family. I stay with my sister or girlfriend Bobbi and make it a point to see other friends. I spend time with my children and grandchildren. Friends that I see and don't see I'm in touch with via email and most recently my Facebook page.

Canton is a wonderful place to live in spite of being listed as one of the top 10 miserable cities. We have great entertainment, restaurants, the Pro Football Hall of Fame, and an Arts District that is second to none. The people in Canton are friendly and definitely made me feel at home when I arrived. Collaboration with social service agencies is superb. It is about the clients and not personal agendas.

Canton, like any other city has its share of crime, some politicians that are self-serving, neighborhoods that need attention, etc. Visit Canton! I think you'll like us!

I pray my book has been a blessing. As Mike Jones, NMT, treats my Occipital Neuralgia, I will document every detail and pray the outcome reported to you in my next book will be one that reads "CURED!"

God bless you.

A GOD SENT WOMAN

God sent Betty Mac to this city.
She is very intellectual and witty.
A visionary with the ability to see.
The positive things that can be.
Eleven years ago she came here on a mission.
Fulfilling her courageous commission.
Canton is far better because she came our way.
Continue to bless her Lord, I pray.
Her faith many times propelled her through,
Trails that would have anchored some of you.
Thank God for this woman of grace.
Who wears a beautiful smile on her face.
She has learned to trust the main source.
As she journeys on her God directed course.
She is one to admire.
Lord grant her utmost desire.
An inductee in God's Hall of Fame.
Multitudes will remember her name.
Written by Michele E. Seymour
December 3, 2009

Betty M. Smith

CONTRIBUTIONS OF $3,000 TO $450,000 DURING MY 10 YEARS WITH MULTI-DEVELOPMENT SERVICES OF STARK COUNTY

Ada C. and Helen J. Rank Charitable Trust
Alcohol and Drug Addiction Services Board
AT & T
Aultman Foundation
Bill Clarke
Charter Bank
Community Building Partnership
City of Canton
Department of Housing and Urban Foundation
Deuble Foundation
Diebold
Dominion East Ohio
Department of Job and Family Services
Federal Emergency Management Assistance
Fifth Third Bank
Flowers Foundation
GAR Foundation
G.E. Capitol
Herbert W. Hoover Foundation
Hoover Foundation
Huntington Bank
JP Morgan Chase
Kaufmann Foundation
Maytag Community Innovation Award
Mental Health Recovery Services Board
Midwest Tennis Association
Motter & Meadows Architects
Neighborhood Based After-School Initiative
Northeast Ohio Tennis Association
Ohio Department of Alcoholism and Drug Addiction Services
Ohio Department of Development

Ohio Department of Education
Paul and Carol David Foundation
Points of Light Foundation
Silk Foundation
Sisters of Charity
Stark County Family Council
Stark County Realtors Association (Have a Heart)
Stark Community Foundation
Suarez Corporation
Timken Foundation
United Way Community Initiative
William and Minnette Goldsmith Foundation

Edwards Brothers,Inc!
Thorofare, NJ 08086
04 June, 2010
BA2010155